BRITISH STUDIES IN APPLIED LINGUISTICS 6

LANGUAGE AND NATION

Papers from the Annual Meeting of the
British Association for Applied Linguistics
held at University College, Swansea
September 1990

Edited by Paul Meara and Ann Ryan

1991
British Association for Applied Linguistics
in association with
Centre for Information on Language Teaching and Research

The maps on pp14-15 are reproduced with permission from the University of Wales Press.

First published 1991
Copyright © 1991 British Association for Applied Linguistics
ISBN 0 948003 94 4

Printed in Great Britain by A McLay & Co Ltd. Cardiff.

Published by Centre for Information on Language Teaching
Regent's College, Inner Circle, Regent's Park, London NW1 4NS

CONTENTS

INTRODUCTION

When we planned the 1990 Annual Meeting of the British Association for Applied Linguistics back in 1989, one of the reasons for choosing the title **Language and Nation** was that it seemed to be a particularly appropriate focus for the papers when the venue for the meeting was to be in Wales. This was one way of acknowledging the special importance of language in a country which has caught the attention of the language world by going some way towards providing an official answer to the needs of its bilingual speakers. It was for this reason that BAAL invited one of the plenary speakers to contribute a paper specifically on "the Welsh question". Colin Williams, in his keynote paper "Language, Nation and Territory" looked particularly at the development of a languge policy in Wales with special reference to historical developments this century and to the current attempt by Dyfed County Council to find a solution over a large geographical area with mixed English and Welsh settlement patterns.

But the theme "Language and Nation" was intended to invite papers from any corner of the field - and little did we realise how topical the subject would prove to be! At the time of the meeting in September 1990, the demolition of the Berlin Wall was a fact of history, with the full unification of Germany already under way; this gave rise to several papers on "the German question", represented here by papers from Stevenson, Barbour and Hoffmann. At the time of going to press (August 1991) we are acutely conscious of the problems which face a disintegrating Soviet Union, and of the part which language has played in maintaining the separate identies of its constituent republics; it remains to be seen whether the path to full nationhood will be made any easier for republics like the Ukraine and Georgia because they have a rallying point (a "standard", as Stevenson calls it) in their own language. Perhaps, like those Russian dolls which nest inside each other, within each political entity there are smaller and yet smaller numbers of speakers of languages longing for their own national independence. But Pachev reminds us that in 1971, out of a total of 132 states examined worldwide, in only 12 were the political boundaries co-terminous with a linguistic boundary. So, to have many languages within one state is the norm rather than the exception, and it requires political skills of a considerable order to handle the potential conflicts. He proposes a sociolinguistic, theoretical framework within which language planners might profitably work.

The language problem in Africa was also the subject of several papers, represented here by Mann and Robinson. This huge multilingual continent produces communities who are not just bi-lingual but often users of three or four local languages with English or French as an accepted lingua franca. While accepting the need for such an international language, Mann outlines a proposal for a language policy in Nigeria which would give increased status to the main local languages (Yoruba, Ibo and Hausa), and Robinson provides detailed field reports on the real use of local languages and French in the Ombessa area of South Cameroon. These give a picture of language politics in action.

Mitchell reminds us that part of the solution must lie in the classroom, and she examines the status of community languages in the National Curriculum, with some welcome notes on practice in Australia and New Zealand where the problem appears to be handled with a sensitivity which the DES might do well to copy. Leung and Franson look at current teaching methods for immigrant children in schools and wonder if we do them a service by plunging them into classrooms to absorb English via a curriculum subject.

We often think of a common language as a unifying principle, but we need only open our newspapers to see the awsome, divisive power of language at work. An artificially created state like Yugoslavia falls apart before our eyes as the corrosive anger of suppressed ethnic groups erupts into violence: nationality, religion, economic inequality, and, undoubtedly, language, in an explosive combination. In its early days, BAAL was largely concerned with English - its form, teaching it, its acquisition by speakers of other languages... How far we have come, when the theme of the Annual Meeting mirrors the concerns of the day so accurately.

Ann Ryan
Paul Meara

University College of Swansea
August 1991.

LANGUAGE AND NATION: Europe

LANGUAGE, NATION AND TERRITORY

Colin Williams
Staffordshire Polytechnic

In Wales, unlike many of our European neighbours, we have been relatively fortunate, in that our predominantly non-violent history of inter-group relations has lessened the potential of language-related conflict leading to threats to state stability and civil war. However, the price for our moderation and accommodation politics in the past has been the severe erosion of our national culture. Today there is a vigorous movement in defence of a separate Welsh identity and culture drawing on a large number of varied and loosely associated interest groups, all of whom claim to be active in the name of the nation.

Analytically we may define these groups and agencies as instruments for language survival. But the socio-political context within which these instruments operate is a changing space. My intention in this paper is to examine some of the tensions engendered for Welsh language reproduction by the scale and pace of change. I am particularly concerned with the role and relevance of territory, as a material context for the construction of a bilingual Wales. I will not deal with the detailed description of these changes (see Williams 1989c), preferring to highlight some implications for language reproduction and national identity in a challenging and ever-changing social order.

Currently we are being asked to acknowledge "The rebirth of history" (Glenny 1990) in many parts of Europe as whole societies grapple with the profound implications of transition in a post-marxist/post-modernist world. I would add that we are also seeing a redefinition of geography as space and place become transformed by technology and the re-organisation of political and social affairs.

In the past the attempt to anchor whole societies to specific places, "to nationalise space", has been a recurrent theme of European socio-political development. It has been a major cause of conflict and warfare which has had a determining influence on the creation of national peoples and on the formation of states. The intimate relationship between a particular territory and its people has been a fascinating theme of social history, capable of being interpreted in a

7

quite different fashion by successive generations of inhabitants. The politicization of territory reached its most intense expression in the nineteenth century's age of nationalism and induced a complex process which Williams and Smith (1983) termed "the national construction of social space". Having achieved an acceptable level of control over their disparate peoples, the leaders of most modern European states sought to induce a situation of national congruence throughout their territories. It was the outcome of the multilayered crises posed by the issues of identity, legitimacy, participation, distribution, and penetration, which structured the relationship between the state and its constitutent peoples. Three consequences flow from the state's attempt to socialise its people through politicizing its territory (Williams and Smith 1983; Williams 1989b). The first is the increase in society's control over and ability to manipulate the environment so as to endow the state with a powerful resource base, infra-structure and communication system. Such environmental manipulation has involved the construction of a new state-centred citizenry, through mass-education, political orientation, conscription and the development of a civic religion focused on statehood, political sovereignty and economic autarchy.

A second consequence has been the "hardening space" which involves the filling out of power vacuums and the utilization of all areas for social benefit and communal power. National leaders, especially in Western Europe, have been unremitting in this task of furthering the state's interests through the active penetration of all of its territory. The modern bureaucratic-territorial state is sufficient testimony of the virulence of the state idea, and of its ability to "unleash a collective energy for development that can utterly transform the environment and deter aggressors" (Williams and Smith, 1983, 513).

A third consequence has been the growing abstraction of the land, that has been given new meaning as the physical and social environment becomes re-interpreted to suit the exigencies of the age. This is evidenced in the return to nature movement, the zest for cultural-linguistic revivals, the penetration of ecological thought into mainstream culture and praxis, and in the pluralism currently evident in post-modern society.

Table 1 presents some structural characteristics of minority nationalism. Here the land and a valued environment figure prominently both as a context for socio-political processes and as a cultural repository for a threatened group identity.

8

Table 1: Some structural characteristics of minority
nationalism.

1: defence of a unique territory, the homeland, and the
protection of a valued envirmoment.

2: defence and promotion of a culture and identity, language,
religion, social existence.

3: resistance to centralist trends and relative powerlessness
over decision-making.

4: perception of exploitation and underdevelopment,
structural discrimination

5: resistance to outsiders, immigrants, settlers, colonisers

6: fear of loss of local dominance and influence expressed
through cultural attrition

7: violent and non-violent expression of ethnic dissent and
discord, escalation of risks

8: group-learning, myth formation, persistent inequalities
shape current ideology and define contemporary identity in
the light of historically significant acts of oppression

9: anti-state, anti-status-quo political action intended to
realise new basis of legitimacy

10: redefinition of the problem situation and of conflict in
the light of most recent events and renewed reforms,
concessions, political accommodations and gains for
beleaguered minority within the dominant system

Hence the significance of resisting deleterious outside
influences in both material and non-material spheres. Hence
also the concern with a comprehensive, but acccurate
definition of the nation and its territory so as to realise a
new basis for political legitimacy, usually in a call for
some form of autonomy. All ten features are present in the
Welsh experience of nationalism. What interests me is how
such realities are created. Who constructs the priorities
and the parameters of the nationalist vision? Let me

illustrate the key role of the intellegentsia in Wales by reference to two influential nationalist thinkers, Saunders Lewis and JR Jones, who between them framed the intellectual justification for making the preservation of the Welsh culture the cornerstone of their nationalist programme.

Creating a sense of time and place

Obviously, nationalism is not an autonomous force and we should be careful not to interpret individual nationalist activists as agents of a transcendent ideology, but rather as part of practical politics. Early nationalist strategists recognised that Wales was divided both linguistically and spatially between a predomnantly Welsh-speaking rural core in the north and west, and a predominantly English-speaking region in the south and north-east, long exposed to systematic anglicisation (Williams, 1989a). In order to promote national consciousness they equated language survival with national unity and freedom. This was to include "....keeping Wales Welsh-speaking....by (a) making the Welsh language the only official language in Wales, and thus a language for all local authority transactions and mandatory for every official and servant of every local authority in Wales: (b) making the Welsh language a medium of education in Wales from the elementary school through to the University." (Jones 1970).

Education and public admnistration were to become the chief agencies for language reproduction in a future Wales, as seen by the early nationalist intellectuals in the 1920s. But theirs was not a narrow conception of their predicamant, as many have subsequently charged. Whilst mainstream opposition politics in Europe was embracing materialistic explanations for the oppression of the people, early Welsh nationalists sought a redefinition of the political order in moral, not materialistic terms. Whilst the majority of nationalist writers at the time turned to the Celtic realm for moral inspiration and contemporary models for imitation in the national struggle, Saunders Lewis sought his authenticity in the Catholic, Latin civilisation of Europe. Lewis, the President of Plaid Cymru, 1926-39, argued that medieval Europe possessed a unity of spirit and of law which nurtured minority cultures because diversity could be acommodated within a universal European civilisation. In his seminal paper, *Egwyddorion Cenedlaetholdeb* (Principles of Nationalism) delivered at Plaid Cymru's first Summer School in 1926, he outlined his conception of Welsh national history which was to be influential in subsequent justiications of party strategy and direction.

Table 2: a summary of Saunders Lewis' interpretation of
         Welsh History (based on Lewis 1926).

ROMAN EUROPE
condition: unity enforced by a dominant Christian, Latin
           civilisation which induced a European moral
           integrity.
result: Minority peoples, though conquered, were elevated
           by sharing a powerful, civilising tradition.

MEDIEVAL EUROPE
condition: the one and indivisible church exercising supra-
           national authority
result: local cultural diversity nurtured and protected
           within a framework of spiritual and legal unity

REFORMATION EUROPE
condition: successive challenges to the universal Christian
           order by individual and institutional interests
result: Church authority denied; the King's sovereignty
           and writ established; the state replaces the
           Church as the supreme sovereign body, leading to
           confusion, disintegration, and the genesis of
           the state's drive towards unitary principles

16th CENTURY NATIONALISM
condition: unification and integration sought within states
           by establishing one government, one language, one
           state law, one culture, one education, one
           religion
result: "the triumph of materialsim over spirituality, of
           paganism over Christianity, of England over
           Wales"

CONTEMPORARY BRITAIN (1926)
condition: imperialistic and Marxist challenges within an
           advanced industrial order.
result: a materialistic spirit of narrow and godless
           nationalism; destroying the individuality of
           Wales

PRESCRIPTION The establishment of a central Welsh authority exercising self-government and guaranteeing the primacy
of the Welsh language in all aspects of public life.

Language survival was the key focus of nationalist praxis, for the nurturing of Welsh was a testimony of Wales's continuing cultural contribution to a common European order. In maintaining the language, the Welsh had kept the faith of an organic nationalism derived from medieval Christendom. Wales's original (hence pure) nationalism was set in sharp contrast to British state nationalism, which emerged in the sixteenth century to challenge the universal moral order of the Church and set the state above both God and His people. Lewis's continentalism (which was to cause him much damage within political circles in subsequent years) was born out of his admiration for classical literature, for several French Catholic contemporaries (including Charles Maurras, leader of Action Française who radicalised W. Ambrose Bebb) and of course, from his own conversion to Catholicism (Lewis, 1986; Jones 1986; Davies, 1985).

Lewis counterposed the twin external forces acting on contemporary Wales, the Empire and the League of Nations. He urged his fellow nationalists to shun the Imperial dream and work to reconstruct a Europe of the nations, in which Wales, along with the other nations of the United Kingdom, would be represented as a free, democratic country and be "Europe's intepreter in Britain".

In this re-orientation of Welsh politics and history Lewis sought to present a mutually exclusive set of alternative identities. One could either be 'truly Welsh' and uphold the national vision of Wales being a co-equal partner in European civilisation and development, or one could deny this view and accept the English position that the United Kingdom was an indivisible state wherein English values and priorities took precedence (Williams, 1988). Lewis sought to legitimise the right of Welsh independence by reference to a common European morality rather than to the constitutional patronage of Westminster and Whitehall.

I have argued elsewhere that if Lewis gave to Welsh nationalism a sense of unbroken historical affiliation with mainstream European civilisation, then JR Jones gave it a sense of place by rooting the national community in the Welsh landscape (Williams, 1989a,b,c). Professor Jones's central thesis was that the mutual interpenetration of land and language creates a people over time, and it was this sense of peoplehood, of identity, which was under severe threat of extinction. "Cydymdreiddiad tir ac iaith"' (the interpenetration of land and language) suggests that a thousand secret chords bind people to the land, and that centuries of continuous occupation confirm the land as the vessel which safeguards and nurtures all cultural traditions. This is not a natural process; it is an experiential act which reproduces itself daily in people's souls and is therefore collectively witnessed in society's commonplace actions - in the naming of mountains and vales, rivers and villages and in the whole iconography of landscape. Language is thus the key to meaning and identity. Consider Jones's imagery:-

In this marriage, and as its foundations, ...we see People, as it were, taking hold of their land and partnering it into the texture of their lives through the intercession of language. They would,as it were, see and handle and love the earth through the mirror of their language" (Jones, 1966:14 my translation).

In lamenting his despoiled Wales, with the cataclysmic weakening of the bond between land and language, Jones argues that the Welsh people are in danger of losing their nationhood. British identity is no substitute for Welsh national identity, for Britishness is false-consciousness. British state ideology persists because it is a necessary means of dealing with the relative lack of state integration and cultural assimilation in Wales. It is the Welsh language which symbolises the continuing struggle for separateness; without it the Welsh would have been absorbed centuries ago into the English state. Britishness is a myth, a self-deception, beguiling and pernicious because it is reproduced systematically and absorbed unconsciously.

The consequence of state ideology is to induce among the Welsh a false premise for their existence, for they are destined to be consigned to play a parasitic role on their neighbour's identity-formation process. The urgent task for the national movement is to disestablish British consciousness in Wales, for the end of Britishness could be the re-birth of Welshness. His writings end with a series of appeals to the politicised youth to protect their separateness, to insist upon their Welshness over and above the appeals of a British identity and to fight for their claim to nationhood. "Eich ysbryd yn unig a'ch cyfyd ac a'ch gesyd i sefyll ar eich traed" (p.59). Together with Saunders Lewis's famous radio broadcast, *The Fate of the Language* (13th February, 1962), JR Jones's call to action spurred on the Welsh Language Society of which he was the leading intellectual voice for the remainder of the decade.

Inexorable decline has characterised the fortunes of the Welsh language in the present century. Both the spatial patterns and social processes of aggregate decline and

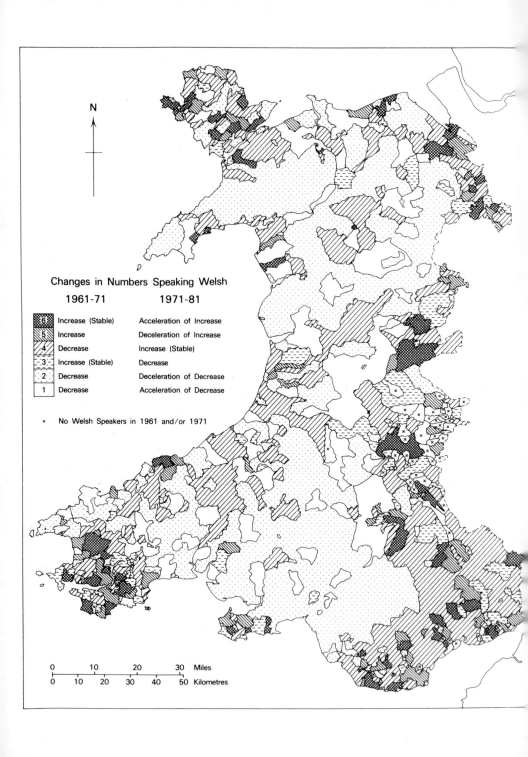

N

Changes in Numbers Speaking Welsh

1961-71	1971-81
6 Increase (Stable)	Acceleration of Increase
5 Increase	Deceleration of Increase
4 Decrease	Increase (Stable)
3 Increase (Stable)	Decrease
2 Decrease	Deceleration of Decrease
1 Decrease	Acceleration of Decrease

×   No Welsh Speakers in 1961 and/or 1971

0	10	20	30	Miles
0	10	20	30	40	50	Kilometres

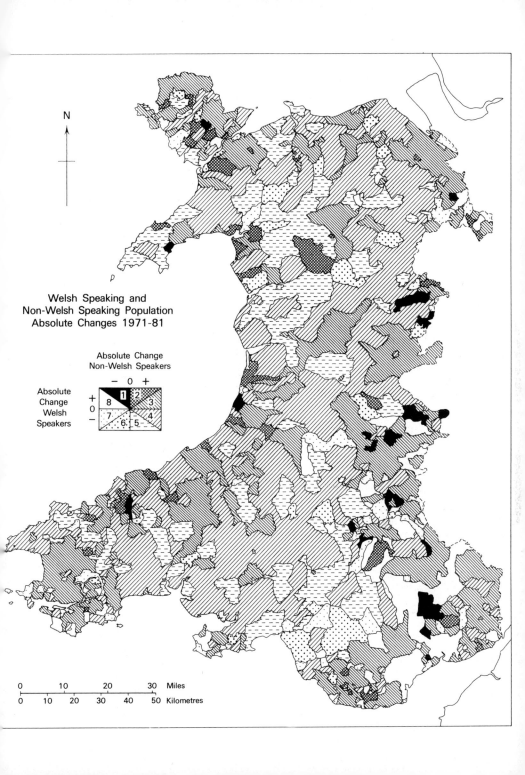

Welsh Speaking and
Non-Welsh Speaking Population
Absolute Changes 1971-81

Absolute Change
Non-Welsh Speakers

Absolute
Change
Welsh
Speakers

	−	0	+
+	1	2	3
0	8		3
−	7	6 5	4

N

0   10   20   30   Miles
0   10   20   30   40   50 Kilometres

limited growth have been extensively documented. One might almost be tempted into thinking that charting the fluctuations in the use of Welsh is the daily pre-occupation of many Welsh people. Certainly within Welsh-speaking circles, particularly in the media, there is an almost paranoic concern with its health. On the one hand this is a natural reflection of the concern and interest with which the language is invested; on the other hand it can lead to a myopic perspective, often involving gross misinterpretations of everyday social issues as primarily linguistic in both origin and consequence.

Census records indicate that at its peak in 1911, the Welsh-speaking population numbered 977,400, of whom 190,300 were monoglots. By 1981 the Census recorded 503,549 Welsh speakers 21,283 of whom were monoglot Welsh although the data should be treated with caution (Williams 1982a). In crude terms this suggests a proportional loss of 25 per cent, from 44 per cent in 1911 to only 19 per cent of the Welsh population by 1981. However, this certainly underestimates the total population of Welsh speakers on two counts. First, it excludes from the analysis the many thousands of Welsh speakers who reside outside Wales. Secondly, there is good evidence to suggest that many Welsh speakers interpret their self-assessed inadequacy to communicate effectively in "standard Welsh" as sufficient reason not to claim an ability to speak, read and write in Welsh on the official census. The corresponding spatial pattern of this decline since 1911 has been extensively documented, and Pryce and Williams (1988) provide a summary of the research findings. We may note here only the salient features of this pattern. First there has been a steady erosion of the once undifferentiated western heartland (Y Fro Gymraeg) which is now redefined as a series of fragmented nuclei - Ynys Mon, Llyn and Arfon, Merionydd-Nant Conwy, rural Dyfed and industrial south-east Dyfed/West Glamorgan (Carter, 1988). Secondly, there has been a corresponding increase in both the absolute and proportionate terms of Welsh speakers in former long anglicised areas of the industrial north-east and south-east of Wales. The reasons for this growth are well documented (Williams, 1982b; 1984; Aitchison and Carter, 1985). They include population redistribution in Wales, the more diverse occupational opportunities in industrial regions, the growth of an indigenous and successful Welsh-medium education sector and the learning of Welsh by many in adulthood. Thirdly the changing geography of the language has necessitated a reformulation of geolinguistic analysis so as to take account of institutional factors, behavioural orientations and a changing socio-economic context. Finally, this fragmentation and drift militates against the adoption of a uniformly designated territorial language region within which citizen rights and the primacy of Welsh may be specified and sanctioned (Williams, 1982a,b; 1985). This is a theme to which we shall return.

Territory and language reproduction

The basis of the nationalist policy on language has been that Wales is an integral unit and should not be subject to social or territorial differentiation in terms of recognisisng language rights. In consequence there have been few serious proposals to limit the full use of Welsh to only predominantly Welsh-speaking regions, i.e. Gwynedd and Dyfed. This is not to deny the existence of a persistent ambiguity within the the nationalist and language movements as to the role of the heartland in public policy and planning considerations. Periodically there are calls to buttress heartland areas and to concentate resources on the most Welsh-speaking communities, rather than to offer a fragmented nationwide service as in, for example, the bilingual education sector.

As a result of a wide variety of factors which characterise modern society many individuals are now more autonomous, seeking language contiguity without necessarily expecting such interaction to take place within geographic contiguity. Processes such as the in-migration of non-Welsh speakers, language shift, mixed marriages, the revolution in tele-communications and access to the media, have reduced the probability of inhabiting settled Welsh-speaking communities as a local majority. In consequence the sheer influence of a local mass of Welsh speakers predisposing a new generation to reproduce the language and the culture can no longer be taken for granted.

Must we perforce conclude that place and territory are no longer significant? Do we accept the post-modernist critique in its entirety and toll the deathknell of Welsh? The devaluation of place and the marginalisation of space as operative social variables does not lessen the significance of territory. Rather it forces us to recognise the inherently more complex role it plays in the articulation of language rights and in the provision of language-related service, which these rights are meant to enshrine in the fabric of the state. This is not to deny the reality of the post-modern landscape. Soja (1989) drawing on Giddens for a systematic account of the spatiality of social life, views the intelligible lifeworld as a "multilayered system of socially created nodal regions, a configuration of differentiated and hierarchically organised locales". His post-modernism consists of four dimensions: "an epochal transition in material life and in critical thinking, a reflection of totalising discourse, and a search for a new language of representation". In Wales part of this transition reflected in material life was the opening up of previously relatively closed cosmologies and the deconstruction of a culture support system based upon a rural, community based infra-structure. So long as the culture was in the ascendancy change could be accommodated in particular regions. Once the culture was under threat on all fronts then most change was perceived as necessarily harmful and this led to an inherent conservatism which assumed that the language could only be rooted in one particular socio-economic niche. Clearly this niche was largely dependent upon the institutional support of late nineteenth century Liberal Conformity for its material and spiritual sustenance. Once modernisation and secular-isation had eroded such support the language was exposed and faced a rootless, confused future. The situation was bad enough in a modern context, now that we have entered a post-modern period then the language is in extremis, or so the argument would have us believe.

Language survival

Although initially designed to characterise the Welsh situation, table 3 is capable of being extended to cover several other European ethno-linguistic minorities. Stage one, **idealism**, refers to the period 1890-1945, when originally Cymry Fydd, and more effectively Plaid Cymru, sought to anchor the fate of the language to the future of the nation. Stage 2, **protest**, refers to the period 1945-1975, when Cwmdeithas yr Iaith Gymraeg in particular highlighted the perceived inequalities in the state's treatment of English and Welsh. Non-violent protest and a strong dose of counter-culture, counter-state rhetoric were the twin expressions in Wales of wider disenchantment with the bureau-cratic, territorial state in advanced industrial societies. Stage three, **legitimacy**, refers to the period 1975-1985 when the language rceived a number of significant boosts in its statutory and practical implementation, in the articulation of language rights consequent to the Welsh language Act of 1967 and in the public's greater acceptance of societal bilingualism. Stage four, **institutionalisation**, refers to the contemporary period, when new domain construction in the para-public sector of the state and local authority has created new employment and socialisation oportunities. Stage five, **parallelism/normalisation** should characterise the next generation's experience as a comprehensive reflection of bilingualism in most aspects of daily life.

Table 3: Language Survival: five foci of social pressure for language change

idealism the construction of a vision of a fully re-habilitated "threatened" language: this is the issue of making language and nation coterminous

protest mobilising sections of the population to agitate for a social reform/revolution in the promotion of the lesser- used language

legitimacy securing a generalised acceptance of the normalcy of exercising language rights in selected domains

institutionalisation ensuring that the language is represented in key strategic agencies of the state: the law, education, and public adminsitration

parallelism/normalisation extending the use of the language into the optimum range of social situations: the private sector, entertainment, sport and the media

It is evident that the institutionalisation of Welsh necessarily invokes quite different evaluations of the relationship between nation, language and territory. Nowhere is this more evident than in the bilingual education policies of several Welsh counties.

A contemporary illustration of the tensions engendered between language rights, local majorities and group socialisation is provided by the recent controversy over Dyfed's bilingual education policy. We know that schools are the critical agency in language reproduction in Wales and that education is central because it serves as the basis for ideological formation and legitimisation of values and positions within society (G Williams 1987). In Dyfed's case there has been a growing recognition that changing demographic and linguistic realities consequent to increased in-migration by non-Welsh speakers into predominantly Welsh-speaking areas has posed difficulties at all levels because of the mixed language abilities and backgrounds now found in many primary schools.

Formed by local government reorganisation in 1974, Dyfed inherited the varied geolinguistic character of its former counties, Pembroke Cardigan and Carmarthen. Three years later it formulated its new language policy based upon Cardigan's established education policy, but recognising that in the more anglicised parts of the new county bilingualism would not be the operative goal. In the early eighties it was becoming clear that the bilingual policy was ineffective for the following reasons:

> (a) it did not reflect existing language patterns; (b) it did not reflect the varying geographical divisions of Dyfed; (c) it was too ambiguous and could be interpreted in a number of diferent ways: (d) children who commenced school with English as their first language did not achieve bilingualism by eleven (with some exceptions) but children who commenced school with Welsh as their first language did become bilingual - but there were different expectations of the two groups (Dyfed County Council, 1990).

Concern that initially English speaking children were definitely not becoming bilingual led to the development of an amended language policy which took into consideration the existing language trends, the geographical divisions, the educational desirability of bilingualism in Dyfed and the the discussions on the role of Welsh in the National Curriculum. In consequence of this review Dyfed's educational provision was sub-divided into three territorial patterns: (a) those areas which were traditionally Welsh-speaking; (b) urban areas which had been substantially anglicised for a long time; (c) South Pembrokeshire which had always been outside any bilingual policy (Dyfed County Council, 1990).

The county's representatives were keen to emphasise that these three policies within one overall policy were designed to meet different language situations, for it was the areas which were categorised initially and not individual schools. Subsequent ratification by all the various levels of authority from individual school Governing Body to the full County Council, led to the implementation of the revised schools policy in September 1989. Those children in school would continue with the previous policy whilst children entering the school after 1989 would be taught in accordance with the amended language policy.

Opposition to this amended policy emerged with the formation of Education First, whose chairperson Blodwen Griffiths voiced the fears and apprehension of parents who claimed their children were now being force-fed Welsh in school. Members of Education First were careful to stress that they were not opposed to formal teaching of Welsh in overwhelmingly Welsh-speaking districts of the county, but that their opposition was based upon a recategorisation of schools with the result that parents who did not anticpate their children receiving such instruction through Welsh were now faced with a different language regime in many schools. They were thus simply exercising their democratic right by pressing for a reversal of the policy and/or moving children out of a particular school to one which reflected the home background of the parents.

The key issue was the role of Welsh in Category A schools (where Welsh is the main but not the only medium of instruction), a primacy confirmed by the Education Committee in its meeting of 20th December 1990. The Secretary of State for Wales, having been petitioned by Education First, saw no reason to act in regard to the Authority's language policy. Dyfed County Council now intend to allow a period of stability so as to meet the requirements of the National Curriculum and disseminate more specific information to interested parties on its particular policy in all three categories (Dyfed County Council, 1991). However, we may draw out certain implications for our main theme from this case study.

In societies which are increasingly conscious of the need to provide public services in more than one official language, e.g., Canada, Belgium, Finland or Wales, there is often a tension between the functional provision of public services and the formal organisation of territorial-based authorities charged with such provision. This leads to language-related issues being publicly contested as each new domain is penetrated by the formerly disadvantaged language. Dyfed County Council has, in effect, chosen to safeguard the collective territorial rights of Welsh-speakers in its Category A designation, over and above the individual personality and rights of non-Welsh speakers whose educational rights will only be fully met by relocating themselves elsewhere in the County. Without such protection it is doubtful whether local language majorities in the heartland region can ever hope to maintain the primacy of Welsh in the public sphere, let alone extend such rights into the private sector. Thus the policy and planning decisions of Dyfed, Gwynedd and other councils are more significant today than ever before. They not only institutionalise the use of Welsh in the new domains but become the key instruments for changing the relationship between the autonomous individual and the local state. By implication they have significant scope for transforming Welsh into a language of power, or establishment positions, in short, of local government, a transition that would have been unthinkable barely thirty years ago. By extension they are also responsible for changing our conception of the nation and of the utility of both Welsh and English in tandem. Formal language planning is beginning to be realised in Wales by local and national agencies, but the context of such planning is no longer judged in domestic British terms. Increasingly changes within Welsh society as they relate to minority group rights, language reproduction and national redefinition are framed in European or global terms and are to be seen as part of several international trends to allow for greater cultural pluralism within the world system.

Finally if we change the scale of the analysis and concentrate upon wider European currents we may speculate that the relationship between language, nation and territory will be further changed by the evolving European Community. Many non-state nations, such as Wales, initially expressed anxiety over the construction of a supra-national European Community, for they feared that it would exasperate existing core-periphery inequalities in well established nation states. Indeed one of the prime reasons given for the ethnic revival in the 60s and 70s was the rising alienation many felt as power and decision-making was increasingly concentrated in centres which were perceived as being distant, irresponsive and undemocratic. Today, although that fear is still prevalent, it is countered somewhat by a new re-alignment of Federalists, Liberals, Nationalists and Ecologists who together seek to redraw the political maps of Europe. Their twin aims are to protect the diversity of European culture and to re-enfranchise the citizenry in a future federated Europe. The politics of exclusion of the post-enlightenment age would become the politics of inclusion.

Like the European Green parties, the Socialists, Social Democrats and the reformed Communists have all made calls for a decentralisation of institutions in Europe. As John Hume MEP has argued, the issue of preservation of minority cultures and the development of regional economies poses the fundamental question - "What sort of Europe do we want?". He suggests that the tide has turned so that Europe is becoming much more comprehensive in its unity because it values its regional and cultural diversity (while working for a convergence of living standards) of economic, social and cultural rights. Such a unity in diversity would truly fulfill the highest ideals of the founding fathers of the European Community by removing one of the major causes of human conflict - the non-recognition, undervaluing, neglect and even elimination of the identity of peoples (An Grupa Soisialch, 1988).

Only time will tell whether a Federal Europe of the Nations will be constructed, but the process of creating European-side institutions has already had an impact on the smaller language communities. Let me itemise some of the salient issues without comment.

1: A recognition that within a wider European context, many previously discriminated languages can share a revised status and increased utilitly because of their contribution to the common European heritage, of which more than 50 million citizens speak a lesser-used language.

2: The establishment of a network of official, semi-official and voluntary agencies dedicated to furthering the interests of lesser-used languages speakers, notably the European Bureau for Lesser Used Languages.

3: A recognition that goodwill and charity are no guarantees for the survival of minority cultures; an admixture of purposive legislation, language reform and regional panning offer a more holistic interpretation of languge planning.

4: A specification of the rights and obligations of both language community and host state in respect of public recognition, public expenditure and public responsibility for cultural and minority economic affairs. This operates at all levels, from parish decisions to resolutions of the European Community and the Council of Europes's Charter on Regional and Minority Languages.

5: A willingness to pool experience and expertise from within the lesser-used languages communities so as to improve their common predicment ad disseminate good models of cultural reproduction in selected domains.

6: A recognition of the need to reformulate the ideo-logical rationale for bilingualism and multilingualism in an integrated Europe, with a subtle but profound shift away from a preservationist perspective to a more utilitarian, develop-mental perspective on maintaining multilingualism. This is particularly so in situations where the minority straddles international frontiers, eg., Catalan, Eusquerra, Slovene.

7: A clearer understanding of the democratic potential of new information technology in promoting the lesser-used languages through print and vision, especially in education, broad-casting and information systems (Williams, 1990).

Conclusion

In an age of super-computers, where within a few years capacities to process data will be a thousand times what they are today, we can seriously talk of "artificial reality" enabling us to carry out difficult and dangerous experiments by proxy computer simulation. Technology serves to liberate and simultaneously re-imprison the human condition placing new and more stressful demands on our collective ability to cope and adapt. At one end of this global spectrum of adaptation a small, but significant experiment in national re-orientation is taking place in Wales. But this is no artificial reality; it is a complex, dynamic and often frustrating social process of adjustment. Too often in the past the fortunes of the language have been left to free market forces and to an often unresponsive state apparatus. The beginnings of state supported restitution of Welsh culture are in the process of being constructed. The theme of much of my writings in the past has been that at the very time the institutionalisation of Welsh has been realised in selected domains, the territorial retreat of Welsh is reaching a crisis point in the heartland and has not yet spread sufficiently to create significant majorities else-where within Wales. We are thus at a very delicate juncture in that troubled relationship between language, nation and territory. The predconditions of a healthy bilingual and bicultural Wales which are currently being constructed, offer a more promising prospect than has existed for many decades.

I certainly hope this is the case. We surely deserve more of life than to be consigned to history as having taken part in a valiant but futile experiment in putting off the inevitable extinction of a separate culture. For some the struggle for Welsh is itself a meaning-seeking movement, a search for identity and fulfillment. I am afraid my involvement is far more prosaic. It just happens that by an accident of birth I inherited a way of looking at the world and at myself in that world, which for good or worse is now mine own also. At the very least I would argue that the right to existence is what the language struggle represents, a right so powerfully defended in all four quarters of the earth today. If pushed, I might also admit that the struggle adds a certain frisson to daily life precisely because neither my nation nor my language can be taken for granted, for that right to existence is still conditional.

REFERENCES

AITCHESON, J and H CARTER. 1985. *The Welsh Language, 1961-1981*. Cardiff: The University of Wales Press.

AN GRUPA SOISIALACH. 1988. *An Ghaeilge agus Teangacha Eile islu Usaide san Eoraip*. Mid-Ulster:SDLP.

CARTER, H . 1988. *Culture, Language and Territory*. Cardiff: BBC Wales Annual Radio Lecture, 5-43.

DAVIES, DH. 1985. *The Welsh Natonalist Party, 1925-45*. Cardiff: The University of Wales Press.

GLENNY, M. 1990. *The Rebirth of History*. London: Penguin.

JONES, JR. 1970. *Tros Gymru*. Swansea: Ty John Penry.

JONES, MP. 1986. Yr Awel o Ffrainc. *Y Traethodydd*, July.

LEWIS, S. 1926. *Egwyddorion Cenedlaetholdeb*. Cardiff: Plaid Cymru.

LEWIS, S. 1986. *Ati, Wyr Ifainc*. Cardiff: University of Wales Press.

PRYCE, WTR and WILLIAMS CH. 1988. Sources and methods in the study of language areas: a case study of Wales. In: CH Williams (ed) *Language in Geographic context*. Clevedon: Multilingual Matters.

SOJA, E. 1989. *Post-modern geographies: the reassertion of space in critical social theory*. New York: Verso.

WILLIAMS, CH. 1982a. Separatism and the mobilisation of Welsh national identity. In: CH Williams (ed) *National Separatism*. Cardiff: The University of Wales Press.

WILLIAMS, CH. 1982b. The spatial analysis of Welsh culture. *Etudes Celtiques*, 19,283-322.

WILLIAMS, CH. 1982c. Language planning and minority group rights. *Cambria* 9,61-74. Reprinted in an expanded version in: I Hume and WTR Pryce (eds) 1986 *The Welsh and their country*. Llandyssul: Gower Press.

WILLIAMS, CH. 1984. Ideology and the interpretation of minority cultures. *Political Geography Quarterly*, 3,105-125.

WILLIAMS, CH. 1988. Minority nationalist historiography. In: RJ Johnston et al. (eds) *Nationalism, Selfdetermination and Political Geography*. London: Croom Helm.

WILLIAMS, CH. 1989a. The Anglicization of Wales. In: N Coupland (ed). *English in Wales: diversity, conflict and change*. Cleveland: Multilingual Matters.

WILLIAMS, CH. 1989b. The question of national congruence. In RJ Johnson and P Taylor (eds). *A World in Crisis?* Oxford: Basil Blackwell.

WILLIAMS, CH. 1989c. New domains of the Welsh language: education, planning and the law. *Contemporary Wales*, 3, 41-76.

WILLIAMS, CH and AD SMITH. 1983. The national construction of social space. *Progress in Human Geography*, 7,502-518.

Williams, G (ed). 1987. The sociology of Welsh. *International Journal of the Sociology of Language*, 66.

note
I am grateful to Mr Dyfrig Davies, Language Adviser, Dyfed County Council Education Department, for providing me with details of the County's educational policy and accompanying documentation.

DEUTSCHLAND   EINIG   VATERLAND?   CULTURAL   AND   LINGUISTIC
PERSPECTIVES ON GERMAN UNITY

Patrick Stevenson
University of Southampton

The French writer François Mauriac once said "I love Germany
so much I'm glad there are two of them" (cited in an
interview with former French Foreign Minister, Michel Jobert
in Der Spiegel, 37/1987). Since October 1990 this has no
longer been the case and in the 11 months it took for the
peaceful November revolution of 1989 to result in the
dissolution of the two post-war German states, a great deal
of comment and speculation was published in the world's media
regarding the political and economic consequences of the
momentous development.

This   paper   will   attempt   to take stock of the "German
Question" from the perspective of what social historians call
the questione della lingua, understood here not in the narrow
sense of the competing claims of different dialects, but in
the more general sense of the complex relationships between
language, politics and power. Gramsci (1985) maintained that
every time the language question raised its head this was a
sign that other social and cultural changes were afoot and
this paper is part of such a process.   The latest radical
restructuring of the German people is a good opportunity to
assess the importance of language in determining the shape
and the nature of "Germanness", both in the past and the
future.

The main object of the paper will be to examine the
ideological mobilisation of "the German language" in the
interests of fostering and developing a German national
consciousness to support   the   idea   of   Germany as an
einig Vaterland (united fatherland). This will entail loking
first at ninteenth century debates on language in Germany and
the emergence of a German nation as a primarily linguistic
community predicated on the supposed equivalence of Sprache,
Volk and Nation, and then considering the consequences for
the current situation of making language (and especially
linguistic   standardisation)   the   predominant   cultural
phenomenon. The mutual determination of language and nation
is not a new topic. In particular, linguistic convergence
has long been seen as a counterpart to the focusing   of
political power, and founding national languages is as much a

part of the consolidation of power as the founding of nations (Coulmas, 1985). The concern here will therefore be to see what is of special interest about the German situation and how it might illuminate some of the more general issues coming under the rubric of "language and nation".

The most conspicuous irony of the demise of the ruling regime (Socialist Unity Party of Germany) was that it should have come at the end of the year in which both German states celebrated their 40th anniversaries. While the official positions of the two states remained quite distinct, with the GDR vigorously promoting its independence as a socialist state and the FRG maintaining its constitutional position as a provisional arrangement pending the "re-unification" of the German peoples, the general tenor of discussion on both sides reflected the growing public acceptance of the status quo. In the space of virtually two generations a separate state (if not yet national) consciousness had developed in East and West. Few voices would have dissented from Coulmas's view:

> "As a result of World War II, the (near) identity of language, state and nation - that is, the fictitious ideal of linguistic nationalism - has been destroyed in Germany." (Coulmas, 1990a)

Even Peter Alter qualifies his prophetic assessment of the situation in the GDR

> "Sooner or later it (the GDR leadership) will have to square up to the challenge of Ernest Renan's famous definition of the nation - a daily plebiscite"

by predicting that non-violent re-unification was highly unlikely (Alter, 1989).

Yet within a matter of weeks the view that a single state uniting the territory and people (although neither of these terms is uncontroversial in this context) of the FRG and the GDR was somehow "natural" and would acknowledge the existence of a sinlge Geman nation had established itself as the orthodox position on both sides. The long-running dispute over the inheritance of German culture and the right to speak for the German people, embodied in the terms *Allein vertretungsan sprach* (claim to sole representation) - staked by the FRG and *Alleinvertretungsanmassung* (unjustified claim to sole representation) - GDR's rejection of the FRG position, was apparently swept aside. And with it at a stroke will disappear a small but flourishing academic cottage industry that has analysed and debated the development of supposed linguistic differences between East and West German. (Clyne 1984; Barbour and Stevenson 1990).

Thus the "German Question" as it has re-emerged since November 1989 might be seen in terms of reconciling these two conflicting positions, the acceptance of the evolution and maturity of the two Geman states versus the almost atavistic belief in some kind of primordial Germanness. Underlying this contradiction is the old problem of identity and the popular slogans like *Deutschland einig Vaterland* that adorned banners in the demonstrations in Leipzig and elsewhere are precisely what have reopened the debate which has raged on and off since the early nineteenth century on the association between language, state, people and nation.

Of the many possible definitions of nation perhaps the most useful and pertinent in the present context are offered by Alter (1989): "The nation-state represents the site where life is led, and endows existence with meaning both in the present and the future....A nation is a social group...which has become conscious of its coherence, unity and particular interests. ...It is constituted by the social group's consciousness of being a nation or of wanting to be one, and by their demand for self-determination."

According to this view there may be any number of constituent criteria in the determination of a "nation" such as shared language, culture or origins, but the crucial notion is consciousness. The long tradition of highly localised loyalties in Germany impeded the development of a widespread political consciousness of a German nation in Alter's sense until the early years of the 19th century, so that at that stage not only was there no German nation-state but the prerequisite for it was also lacking in the minds of its people.

The problem confronting intellectuals who sought some kind of *Ersatzreligion* to fill the political and moral vacuum created in the aftermath of the French Revolution and the dissolution of the Holy Roman Empire was the lack of an emblem or flag around which to unite the people (von Polenz, 1990). England and France had both a centralised state and a standardised language associated with it for a long time, and even Italy could point to a national language going back to the fifteenth century, even if very few Italians could understand or use it (Scaglione 1984). By contrast, in Germany until the late 18th century there were at least two language questions: not just the debate over what form a standardised variety of German should take, but whether to use any form of

German at all rather than Latin or French in certain public contexts. For example, although Leibniz pleaded the cause of using German in academic and cultural contexts he did not practise what he preached in most of his own work, and it was considered dangerously radical for Thomasius to have the temerity to lecture in German rather than Latin at Leipzig University in 1687 (Scaglione, 1984).

Against this background, it is perhaps less surprising that a kind of complaint tradition developed in the first half of the nineteenth century which, while identifying the German language as the one unifying bond of the German people, bemoaned the lack of a common language among the educated elite. The important point here is not the observable reality of a standardised form but rather public conscious- ness. So, for example, Kolbe (1818) maintains that the mother tongue is the voice of the nation's soul, and that language and literature are the only common bond or fixed point on which public spirit and patriotism could be focused, though he also complains that this view is not shared by the statesmen or the scholars of the day. As late as 1846 complaints were being voiced that the nation was being hampered by the lack of a general language of education.

Much of what was written in this vein was an expression of the older rationalist/authoritarian approach to langugae that sought to rediscover some kind of ideal original state, while at the same time aiming to fix the form of the language in a uniform and stable way through dictionaries and grammars that would have the stamp of authority. Similar moves were afoot in 18th century England (Swift 1712; Johnson 1755). For a critique of "enbalmed" uniform varieties cf Williams (1961).

However, this view was then confronted by one that was more in step with a world which in the last decade of the 18th century had seen how rapidly and radically social change can occur. Herder's conception of language as an essentially changeable product fostered the view that languages were naturally developing organisms that derived their peculiar nature from the particularity of the *Volk*. Humboldt (1830/35) and Jahn (1810) even considered the cultivation of the "mother tongue" to be a necessary quality of humanity. This position appears to be predicated on the belief that both language and nation are given facts, and that nation logically precedes language, the latter being an expression or concrete manifestation of the former. It is therefore difficult to see how this can be reconciled with our contention that there was no widespread sense of nationhood in Germany until it was constructed, as it were retrospectively, on the basis of a shared language. However, the distinction between Staatsnation and Kulturnation (Meinecke, 1969; von Polenz 1988, 1990) is important here, as it can account for the role of language as an ideological vehicle in generating a national consciousness in Germany.

Staatsnation refers to the bonds of a common political history and so to overtly formal characteristics; Kulturnation is based on a shared cultural heritage and will typically incorporate things like language and literature. Each of these phenomena can exist independently of the other, but also each can contain the other and each may derive from the other. On the one hand, for example, Switzerland could be seen as a single Staatsnation containing several distinct Kulturnationen, while early 19th century Germany or indeed the post-WW2 German states could be regarded a single Kulturnation encompassing several Staatsnationen. On the other hand, it could be argued that England and France existed as Staatsnationen before Kulturnationen developed within their borders, while an Italian Kulturnation had existed for a long time before an Italian state was founded in 1861. A national consciousness is necessary for both types of nation to exist as both are circumscribed by internal common features as well as external differences. The "Nation" that 19th century intellectuals in German refer to is the legacy of hundreds of years of shared cultural experience, mediated not by the formal apparatus of a state but by what was perceived as a shared language. A sense of continuous linguistic tradition was what Fichte (1808) saw as essential to the identity of the Germans in distinguishing them from other peoples. The decisive development in the growth of German national consciousness at this point was the politicisation of the Kulturnation as the intellectual basis for the foundation of a single German Staatsnation, and the key instrument in this process was the language.

However, the fact that the German state which finally emerged in 1871 excluded many German-speakers (especially in Switzerland and Austria-Hungary) while including many non-German speakers, demonstrates the fragility of the equation between the two concepts, and this has implications for the current state of affairs in central Europe. For as Alter argues, political unification in a single state does not guarantee the existence of the nation, because the nation (even in the sense of Kulturnation) is not given but must be constructed; it is not a natural but a synthetic product. This, of course, applies also to standard language varieties, and it is the identification of standardised forms of German with various political entities that has constituted the most significant language question in central Europe since the Second World War.

The collapse of the grotesque attempts in the third Reich to realise through force an absolute correspondence of language group, nation and state clearly marked the discreditation of linguistic nationalism in Gemany. However, 1945 represents more a temporary caesura than a complete break in the tradition of associating language with national identity. In fact, it was a matter of only a few years before the questione della lingua resurfaced in a new guise. Until the 18th century the establishment of a single widely accepted standard written form had been hindered by long-standing regional rivalries, and the striving for national unity in the 19th century had focused on the emblematic function of a "national language"; the debate on the nature and status of the now highly codified standard German formed the battlefield on which the struggle for the legitimacy of the two post-war German states, the inheritors of the the mantle of German culture, was fought.

It is now widely agreed that linguistic differences between what was represented as standard German in the FRG and GDR respectively, were negligible and that the debate taking place on the pages of linguistics journals was of an ideological rather than an academic nature. But the language question has always been both politial and ideological, and attempts by linguists engaging in such debates to present their work as value-free are either naive or disingenuous.

What was going on in this now obsolescent field of academic endeavour was really the resumption of an old battle with a different configuration and different protagonists. The existence of a widely accepted standardised form of German was no longer the issue; now it was a case of who should be the rightful guardian of this massive cultural achievement. In the absence of institutions equivalent to the Académie Française, the battle lines were drawn up in the editorial offices of the rival Duden publishing houses in Mannheim and Leipzig. Until 1954, the series of reference works generically referred to as *Duden* (after Konrad Duden who published his original orthographical dictionary in 1880) were published exclusively by the Bibliographisches Institut in Leipzig. Since then, separate editions have been published in Leipzig (GDR) and Mannheim (FRG). The Leipzig office will presumably be one of the many casualties of the industrial rationalisation brought about by the absorption of the former GDR enterprises into the social market economy of the

FRG. The history of the *Duden* is in itself a significant aspect of the cultural and political construction of German identities since 1871.

The important point in the present context is that participants in this debate were articulating the need to hold onto the belief in the existence of a national language as a national institution. Here, the senses of "standard" as implying on the one hand "a yardstick of quality" and on the other "an identifying symbol, like a flag" combine in the attempt to secure cultural continuity in the midst of political conflict. Language thus provided the bridge to the collective cultural past and an effective way of laying claim to this inheritance was to see German as used in one state as the true correct form and any differences emerging in the German used in the other state as deviations from this. This was, of course, a highly selective undertaking on both sides and often amounted to little more than a trading of unsubstantiated insults: the perpetuation of the Nazis' abuse of the language on the one hand, and the subjugation of the language to Soviet control on the other.

However, with the passage of time after the war this debate passed through a number of phases and with hindsight it can be seen as a kind of barometer of changes in the climate between the two states (Kinne, 1977). In the wake of the crucial moves towards normalisation of relations in the early 1970s, a new consensus began to emerge; this accepted the fundamental integrity of the German language while postulating, in a major break with the tradition of the previous 200 years, distinct national varieties for each of the four main German-speaking states - FRG, GDR, Austria and Switzerland. This progressive proposal, known as the pluricentricity of German (Kloss, 1978; Clyne, 1984), has the obvious appeal of disposing of the old myth of the superiority of *binnendeutsch* usage (i.e., the language of Germany as opposed to that of other German-speaking countries), and at the same time acknowledges the dynamic nature of standard language varieties. For the first time standardisation was seen not as a procedure aimed at fixing a definitive form of the language but as a continuous process or an open-ended project.

This approach also takes account of the differences in identification between the generation of Germans who lived through the war and those generations which grew up in one of the new post-war German states. Writing in *Die Zeit* in 1982, the veteran West German journalist Rudolf Walter Leonhardt wrestles with the problem of identifying his nationality as oppposed to his citizenship (*bundesrepublikanisch* rather than *deutsch*); but the very terms *national* and *Nation* had increasingly become synonymous with either the FRG or the GDR, particularly for the younger generations; each country's football team, for example, was referred to as the *Nationalmannschaft* (national team).

The demolition of the monolithic notion of a single standard German variety was not only a healthy move away from a view of the relationship between language and nation that inevitably carried with it the burden of the immediate past. It also opened the way for a new perspective on the function and status of standard forms in German-speaking countries, and indeed more generally (Ammon, 1990). The analysis of German as a pluricentric language is not at odds with Haugen's (1984) succint formulation of the requirements of a standard variety (minimal variation in form, with maximal variation in function); the extent of linguistic variation between the four national varieties is slight and this of course permits virtually unhindered communication across a wide spectrum of social purposes. However, what it does do is to permit identification between language and people to take place on a less global level, and to assign a different status in different places to what is linguistically a fairly homogeneous phenomenon.

So while in Germany and arguably in Austria, formal standard German may be given primacy in hierarchical terms in relation to other arbitrarily designated varieties on a continuum, it occupies a very different position in the overall linguistic constellation both in Switzerland and in other countries on the periphery of German-speaking Europe. In German-speaking Switzerland, for example, the pragmatic discontinuum between Swiss-German dialects and (Swiss) standard German means that the latter does not enjoy the prestigous status accorded to it in Germany. Dialects are the universal medium of spoken interaction in Switzerland, and the function of the standard variety is more that of a technical register, reserved for specific purposes such as written communication or interaction with German-speaking foreigners. In Luxembourg, standard German, as a language of education and widely used in other spheres of public discourse, has an important role to play in keeping the small state within the German cultural orbit, but the fact that it is only co-official with French and the constitutional status of Luxembourgish as sole national language enable the Luxembourgers to keep both of their larger neighbours at arms length (Newton, 1987).

There is, however, dissent from the pluricentric view and not only from the traditional unicentric camp. Rusch (1989) for example, raises doubts and some fears about the suitability and the wisdom of attaching too much importance to the notion of national language varieties in the establishment of national identities. Apart from the dependency implied in the definition of Austrian nationhood in terms of the German language, he sees potential disadvantages in the codification of an Austrian national variety of German, not only for the international image of the Austrians but also as a dangerous totem around which resurgent Austrian nationalism could unite. The Waldheim affair and regressive steps such as the reform of the bilingual Slovene schools in southern Austria suggest that this fear is not without foundation.

However, this problem is clearly not confined to Austria. The very substantial numbers of speakers of languages other than German within the FRG remained an invisible quantity in a West German state that defined itself more in terms of where it had come from than where it was going to. The social pressures created by the rapid formation of a new Germany are likely to affect these citizens of the dominant partner in the so-called merger of the two post-war states even more than the poor German cousins of the former GDR. If language is mobilised again in the painful process of nation building in Germany it could be an ominous development for all. Germany finds itself now between the decline in importance of the nation-state in Western Europe and the resurgence of so-called ethnic nationalism in Eastern Europe. In these volatile circumstances, the most positive contribution by the Germans might be to replace the historically tarnished concept of the *Kulturnation* with the still more abstract notion of *Kulturgemeinschaft* (cultural community), which might still preserve a sense of cultural continuity without prescribing essential characteristics for a German nation.

My main purpose has been to place the movement towards the unification of Germany in a particular context. The intention was to attempt to trace a common theme through various mutations from the emergence of a German national consciousness in the early years of the 19th century to the present day. This common theme was the changing but always central role of language in the process of determining national and cultural boundaries. The final section points towards rather mixed prospects for the future, but stops short of offering any hostages to fortune by making any predictions about the development of the German Question. What form the *questone della lingua* will take next, as far as

German is concerned, remains to be seen, but there seems little doubt that it will be fertile ground for linguistic research in the years ahead.

REFERENCES

ALTER, P. 1989. Nationalism London: Arnold. Translated from: Nationalismus. 1985. Frankfurt: Suhrkamp.

AMMON, U. 1990. German as an international language. In: Coulmas 1990b.

BARBOUR, JS and P STEVENSON. 1990. Variation in German: a critical aproach to German sociolinguistics. Cambridge: Cambridge University Press.

CLYNE, MG. 1984. Language and society in the German-speaking countries. Cambridge: Cambridge University Press.

COULMAS, F. 1985 Sprache und Staat. Berlin: de Gruyter.

COULMAS, F. 1990. The status of German: some suggestions for future research. International Journal of the Sociology of Language 83,171-185.

FICHTE, J. 1808. Reden an die deutsche Nation. Cited here from W Dieckmann (ed) 1989 Reichtum und Armut deutscher Sprache. Berlin, New York: de Gruyter.

GRAMSCI, A. 1985. Selection from cultural writings. D Forgacs and G Nowell Smith (eds). translated W Boelhower. London: Lawrence and Wishart.

HAUGEN, E. 1966. Dialect, language, nation. American Anthropologist, 68,922-935.

HUMBOLDT, W von. 1830-1835. Ueber die Verscheidenheit des menschlichen Sprachbaues und ihren Einfluss auf die giestige Entwicklung des Menschengeschlechtes. Cited here from Coulmas 1985.

JAHN, FL, 1810. Deutsches Volksthum. Cited here from Dieckmann, 1989.

JOHNSON, S. 1755. A dictionary of the English language. London: Longman.

KINNE,   M. (ed) 1977.   Texte-Ost - Texte-West.   Frankfurt:
Diester-weg.

KLOSS,   H.   1978.   Die Entwicklung neuer germanischer
Kultursprachen seit 1800 Dusseldorf: Schwann.

KOLBE, KW. 1818-1820 Ueber der Wortreichhtum der deutschen
und franzoesischen Sprache. Cited here from Dieckmann 1989.

MEINECKE,   F.   1969.   Weltbuergertum und Nationalstaat ed. H
Herzfeld. Munich: Oldenbourg.

POLENZ, P von.   1988. "Binnendeutsch" oder plurizentrische
Sprachkultur? Zeitschrift fuer germanistische Linguistik,
16,198-218.

RUSCH,   P.   1989.   National vs regional models of language
variation: the case of Austria. Language, Culture and
Curriculum 2,1-16.

SCAGLIONE, A. 1984. The rise of national languges: East and
West.   In: A Scaglione (ed).   The Emergence of National
Languages. Ravenna: Longo Editore.

SWIFT, J. 1712. A proposal for correcting, improving and
ascertaining the English tongue.

WILLIAMS,   R. 1961. The Long Revolution. London: Chatto and
Windus.

LANGUAGE AND NATIONALISM IN THE GERMAN-SPEAKING COUNTRIES

Stephen Barbour
University of Surrey

There are several reasons why it is fitting that BAAL should hold its first conference on the theme "Language and nation" in the year of German unification; the notion that a language is the most important defining characteristic of a nation arises particularly in German thinking. It is in German speaking countries that nationalism has, in 20th century Europe, assumed its most virulent form and it could be argued that nationalism in Europe is now at its weakest among certain sections of the German intelligentsia. I would also argue that the virulence of German nationalism in this century and its well known disastrous results have been a crucial factor in promoting a critical examination of nationalism, and have even helped to foster the view that nationalism is per se a destructive force (Smith, 1983). Given the great significance of German nationalism for the phenomenon of nationalism as a whole, it is important for anyone concerned with the topic to have some understanding of nationalism in the German-speaking countries.

Most of us who have spent our formative years within one particular state have some understanding of social and political forces within that state. When considering other states we may be tempted to assume much more similarity than there really is. Alternatively, when it becomes clear that there are substantially different social and political factors operating, we may assume that citizens of other states are motivated by dark, sinister and irrational forces. The latter view of German politics and society was understandably prevalent in Britain in the immediate post-war period; I thought it had died out among the better-informed sections of our populations, but surprisingly, it seems to have been propounded at a recent briefing for the UK Cabinet.

My aim, then, in this paper is to demystify German nationalism. I shall show, in a brief historical survey, how it arose, why language is such a highly important element in its formation, how it differs from some other European nationalisms, why it has assumed such dangeous forms, and why in my view, it may no longer represent a serious threat to the rest of Europe or the world.

I shall make the customary distinction between *nation* and *state*. A state is of course relatively easily recognised in the contemporary world as a political unit which has certain characteristics, most obviously and trivially a seat in the United Nations. But the further we go back into the past, the more difficult this recognition becomes, until in medieval Europe we really cannot recognise states of the modern kind. A nation is more difficult to define, and indeed we can probably go no further than to say that it is a group of people with a common sense of identity sharing either a common language, or a common "sociocultural pattern or both" (Haarmann, 1983) and often either constituting a state or aspiring to do so. The state is of course, a modern form of organisation; I shall label nation-like human groups in the period before states existed as "peoples". This term is probably also useful for a contemporary group of nation-like character which however does not aspire to constitute a state, for example, the North Frisians in Germany. From a Western European point of view there are many peoples, and even nations, which do not constitute states (for example the Scots), and conversely many states are not nations in any meaningful sense; they frequently comprise a number of nations or peoples (for example, the USSR, or most third-world countries). Often they contain only part of a nation; for example, in the view of many Arabs there is a single Arab nation, divided into a number of states. It is tempting from a Western European point of view to reserve the term "nation-state" for those states, found chiefly in Europe, a majority of whose inhabitants clearly belong to a single nation. This usage would however be seen as unforgivably eurocentric by many citizens of other states, since it is part of the ideology of almost all states that they do constitute a nation, even where, in western European eyes, this seems not to be the case.

In the development of European nations and languages, three periods in history can be seen as particularly significant: the 9th and 10th centuries, the period from the 14th to the 16th centuries and the 19th and 20th centuries (Graus, 1985). In each of these periods developments in the German speaking areas have been distinctive characteristics of German nationalism.

Starting in the age of migration, human groupings formed in Europe bearing names which have continued in use as the names of modern nations, for example the English, the French and the Hungarians or Magyars. These groups were in no sense identical to the modern groups which bear the names, but there is often nevertheless continuity of a kind,

40

particularly linguistic. We can often trace a step-by-step development from a language used at that period, by at least a section of the population concerned, down to a modern language. It is perhaps not justified to use the term "nations" for these groups, since we have little idea of what sense of common identity they had, or whether such a sense, if it existed, extended beyond a small ruling elite. In any case states of the modern kind simply did not exist.

By the 9th and 19th centuries such groupings had formed. We can for instance, talk of an "English people", a "Czech people" and a "Hungarian people" at this period. One of the peoples which had formed was the Franks, a people who occupied roughly northern France, modern Belgium, the south-west of the modern Netherands and the southern half of modern West Germany. They were distinctive in occupying a far greater area than most other contemporary peoples, and in controlling many regions outside their own area of settlement, in fact the area known as the Frankish empire - France, the Low Countries, modern West Germany, Bohemia, the Alps and northern Italy. It was also linguistically divided; in the western areas a Germanic-speaking elite had, by the period in question, gone over to speaking the Romance dialects which developed into modern French, and to which the Latin adjective *franciscus* was by then appplied. In the east a wide variety of Germanic dialects was spoken, the Franks having originally been not a single Germanic tribe, but a confederation. The modern German adjective *frankisch* and its predecessors (translated into English as "Frankonian") is and was used only for some of the dialects concerned; a collective term for the Germanic dialects of the Frankish empire being Latin *theodiscus*, derived from the Germanic precursors of the modern word *deutsch*. At this period *theodiscus/deutsch* was very wide in meaning, and referred first only to language. It was only considerably later that the word was applied to people; it was a learned, not a popular word. It would seem that the people referred to themselves and their language more often using names of smaller former tribal divisions, such as *allemannisch*, from which the French *allemand* is derived.

In the 9th and 10th centuries then, *deutsch* was a term of wide and indefinite meaning, signifying "of the people" as distinct from "of the Latin of the church, administration and learning" and as distinct from the neighbouring Romance languages. It was applied to all of continental and west Germanic speech, and was the precursor of not only German but also Dutch and in fact also used in one extant document to refer to English. There must have been, to judge from the contemorary records, very low mutual comprehensibility between many of the dialects referred to as *deutsch*. (For further detail on the etymology of the word, see Kluge 1967).

One can speculate from all this that those who spoke *deutsch* at this period were a very large, extremely diverse group, much larger and more diverse than other contemporary peoples, and that their coherence arose more from belonging to a single political unit and less from a sense of common heritage. They had only a weak sense of common identity, which was to a considerable extent negatively defined; that is, they were the people who did not speak a Romance language. In the delimitation of other contemporary peoples, language, while important, does not seem to have had the same overriding significance. This untypical position of deutsch arose from its speakers forming the dominant group in by far the largest political unit of the time.

After the 10th century tribal units, peoples or nations no longer formed the primary basis for political units in most of Europe until after the First World War. Under feudalism, and absolutism, which followed it, political units were based upon the territory which a particular monarch or dynasty was able to control, which might or might not roughly coincide with the area inhabited by a people.

Not surprisingly, in view of its size and diversity, the continental West Germanic area became increasingly politically fragmented. In other large areas of Europe where dialects related to each other are spoken, the age of migrations often saw a division into various peoples and languages, and the feudal and absolutist periods could then either bring further divisions in language, or feudal territorial boundaries might reinforce already established language divisions, or might in some cases obliterate them. For example the closely related West Slavonic dialects have given rise to Polish, Czech and Slovak, and the minority languages Cashubian and Sorbian; the Iberian romance dialects have given rise to the Portuguese, Castilian Spanish and Catalan languages.

By the 16th century continental West Germanic had, on the basis of political and economic separation, divided into two languages, Dutch and German. This division is unlike many others in that the two languages are grossly unequal in terms of territory occupied and number of speakers. It is also unusual in that one of the two languages, German, is extraordinarily dialectally diverse, with northern German dialects being much closer to standard Dutch (and perhaps in some ways even to English), than they are to southern German dialects.

These factors led some Germans, even linguists, to suggest that Dutch is a German dialaect, but this is a quite untenable position, as is eloquently argued by Goossens (1976). The word *deutsch* was probably first used as an everyday word to describe their own language by people speaking what we now call *Dutch* (hence the meaning of the word in English), only being popularly applied to German later. However, between the 16th and 19th centuries it gradually disappeared in this sense from Dutch, being replaced by *nederlands*, with *hollands* and *vlaams* also being used popularly in the Netherlands and Belgium respectively. In Dutch the word *duits* now means German and German-speakers no longer usually apply *deutsch* to Dutch.

If we examine the German-speaking area, we find that in the feudal and absolutist periods it becomes first of all highly politically fragmented. Then, very gradually, two states emerge, Austria and Prussia, which progressively gain control over more and more of the German-speaking world.

We saw earlier how the 9th and 10th centuries brought distinctive developments in what was to become German-speaking Europe. The next crucial period of development in European languages and nationalisms, the period from the 14th to the 16th centuries, when standard written languages were established in many areas, also saw a development in German which was different from those taking place elsewhere. Compared with German-speaking Europe, some other areas which developed written standard langauges at this time, such as the Netherlands and England, were relatively linguistically homogeneous. Others like France and Italy were more heterogeneous. What is different in the German case is that a single written standard language developed in a highly heterogeneous area. This area was politically fragmented, and, from the 16th century onwards, also divided on a religious basis between Catholics and Protestants. Religion is, of course, a very important element in the sociocultural pattern which plays a prominent part in nationalism and since the 16th century the Protestant-Catholic divide has been important in divisions betweeen European nations, notably between the British and the Irish, and between the Dutch and the Belgians.

I think the single standard was able to develop for at least three reasons. Firstly, the area where it chiefly arose, eastern central Germany, was linguistically central; its dialects, which contributed more to the standard language than any others, are relatively close to both southern and northern dialects. Had a standard developed based on

43

Bavarian or Austrian dialects, we can be almost certain that it would not have been accepted in the north. Secondly, the unifying political entity of the 9th and 10th centuries, the Frankish Empire, had, remarkably, not entirely disappeared. At least on paper, most of the German-speaking area plus Bohemia and Northern Italy belonged to its successor state, the Holy Roman Empire, which still had some institutional reality. Finally, there does seem to have been some sense of German nationality perhaps of a rather negative kind. In a sense, the Germans were, and still are, those inhabitants of central and north-western Europe who are not anything else - not Scandinavians, Poles, Czechs, Hungarians, Italians, French or Dutch. Indeed, the Protestant reformation in 16th century Germany can be seen partly as a German cultural and national movement against an Italian-dominated church.

The next important period for the development of European nationalisms is the 19th and 20th centuries, the great age of the linguistic nations, during which the ideal of the linguistically-homogeneous nation arose, to be realised very imperfectly, and with numerous contentious areas, at the close of the First World War in 1918 (Hobsbawm, 1990).

Why did linguistic nationalism become so important in this period? It is often seen as part of a much larger process of the social transformation of societies which might be described as "traditional", to ones which have often been called "modern". A crucial element in this process is technological advance, leading to a high level of special-isation in economic life. This in its turn leads to greater interdependence between individuals and groups in society, meaning that hitherto oppressed social groups gain economic leverage and demand a voice in the political process. A political unit in which a large section of the population demands a voice requires representative institutions or parliaments and is clearly easier to operate if there is a shared language. This means that the linguistically homogeneous state is favoured, and in 19th century Europe, linguistically based nations, many of them originating in peoples formed in the 9th or 10th centuries or before, come to demand independence from the feudal or absolutist monarchies which control much of the continent (Prussia, Austria, Russia, the Ottoman Empire). In central and eastern Europe, models are provided by the powerful, rich and advanced western states (Britain, France, the Netherlands, all of which appear to be linguistically homogeneous, although all do in fact have considerable linguistic and sociocultural minorities). Nationalism is, of course, not actually voiced in these terms, but is expressed as the right of a God-given, "natural" nation to sovereignty, a nation justified by myths of common descent. In the more developed parts of Europe, including some German-speaking areas, nationalism also becomes important for another reason: the growing complexity of economic life uproots many people, both the socially mobile, and those who leave the land to seek work in industry, who lose the emotional security of a primary village community. They then seek solidarity within a larger, more abstract unit, such as the nation (Smith, 1983).

In the German-speaking area we might have seen a movement simply demanding that each of the many absolutist states into which it was divided introduce representative parliamentary institutions, but instead the movement to sweep away absolutism was generally pan-German. An important reason for this was that many of the units were so small, and had such erratic boundaries, determined partly by dynastic considerations, that they were a real impediment to economic life in an industrialising epoch, and so a strong movement arose simply to abolish them. In short, many of the states were seen simply as unnatural creations of absolutism, or of French intervention, to be removed by a popular uprising. Very important too was the feeling that fragmentation enabled the absolutist princes to remain in power, and that only united action by the entire German people would be strong enough to sweep them away.

What we see then are powerful forces furthering German nationalism, but at the heart of that nationalism, little more than a standard language spoken by a tiny minority of the population, superimposed on a group of related but highly divergent dialects with often almost no mutual comprehensibility. There was also a sense of negative nationalism: that to be German was at least not to be anything else.

In the 19th and 20th centuries therefore, German speakers have, for strong and compelling reasons, sought to bolster nationalism with an inherently weak foundation, inventing, for example, on a pseudo-scientific basis, myths about master-races, such as the Aryans, where there was no traditional myth of national origins. German philosophers such as Fichte, Herder and Wilhelm von Humboldt led the way in stressing the importance, even the overriding importance of languaage in nationalism (Inglehart and Woodward, 1977; Coulmas, 1985). Fichte, Schegel, Schleiermacher and others were also prominent in presenting the nation as a "natural" phenomenon, thus placing it beyond sceptical enquiry, perhaps conscious at some level or other that the German nation, if examined too closely, might turn out to have a rather fragile basis (Smith, 1983). It is interesting that Marxism, which of course developed out of earlier German traditions, sees the development of nations as a necessary stage in human history.

The insistence on a "natural" basis for German nationality has led to the use of the principle of descent as the main criterion for determining German citizenship. This is not only potentially racist, but also causes severe administrative difficulties, since it is very hard to prove or disprove the nationality of someone's remote ancestors. The idea of the common descent of any nation is in any case a very difficult principle to operate in law, since descent is almost always, as Oeser (1984) points out, a matter of tradition as much as biology.

The period 1871 to 1945, from the unification of Germany to the defeat of Hitler, is almost an object lesson in the dangers of nationalism. The Second Reich created in 1871 was at once too large, rich and powerful for the other European powers to tolerate, so that they looked from the outset for a chance to cut it down to size. At the same time it was not large and powerful enough to satisfy the more extreme nationalist sentiments which had been created within it; it excluded Austria and a number of other areas of considerable German-speaking population, notoriously, the Sudetenland in Czechoslovakia. It did not have an extensive colonial empire, which, it was felt, every great power must possess. Perhaps more importantly it contained a very large, rootless insecure population in its urban centres, as a result of extremely rapid industrialisation in the second half of the 19th century.

There is, I think, no question that, at least until 1945, the German speaking population of the old Austro-Hungarian Empire considered its nationality to be German, and shared in cultural political movements in Germany, as Hitler's career shows, and as we read in Hobsbawm's personal account of his childhood experiences in Austria (Hobsbawm 1990). When German nationalism was severely checked by the defeat of 1918, the consequences were, within a few years, quite disastrous. The Nazis embarked on a war of conquest to unite all speakers of the German language within one state, espoused the notion of German national superiority to the extent of sweeping aside other nations which stood in its path, and bolstering the intrinsically rather weak basis of German nationalism with absurd racialist myths, exploiting an anti-Semitism which has been present in most Christian countries at some level or other.

The defeat of 1945 produced an utterly new situation. Austria has now become quite separate, being able to present itself to the outside world as an innocent victim of fascist aggression; this is historically quite incorrect, and ignores the fact that Hitler himself was an Austrian. But since 1945 Austria has not on the whole wished to be German and has developed its own nationalism, which is heavily derived from earlier German nationalism. Austria has not experienced the large-scale revulsion against German nationalism seen in Germany.

In Germany itself, this rejection of nationalism has been a notable feature of the attitudes of an important secton of the academic and political elite. In West Germany it reached a peak in 1968 with the revolt by students against almost everything their parents' generation believed in. These days the German intelligentsia, both east and west, are in my opinion less nationalistic than their counterparts in other European countries such as Britain.

What of the current situation? It seems to me that it has certain worrying features. Firstly, nationalism of even quite an aggressive kind is not dead in Germany; it is, in my experience, quite strong for example among working-class people, particularly those who are economically insecure, and the economic insecurity of East Germans is currently considerable. Not only are economic factors important, but there is also a tendency on the part of some to disbelieve what they have been told about the German past. This produces comments such as : "The concentration camps were invented by the allies", or "We did awful things, but then so did the others; we just haven't been told about them". Some of the scepticism of older people is understandable in view of the crudity of some allied post war propaganda, which tried to persuade Germans that they were inherently more evil than other people. One can also understand some scepticism among the population of East Germany: they know the old GDR government lied to them about many things. There is some feeling that perhaps what they said about the war and fascism was lies too.

Another worrying feature is the persistence of the principles of descent in determining nationality. It means on the one hand that native-speakers of German born in Germany cannot automatically claim citizenship if their parents are, say, Turkish immigrant workers. On the other hand, so-called ethnic Germans from the Soviet Union, many of whom do not speak German, and who are not therefore German in the eyes of most of the indigenous population, can automatically claim citizenship if they can show German ancestry, however remote. In a situation of intense competition for housing, the people who do not appear to be German can be targets of nationalistically-inspired aggression.

On the positive side, I have already mentioned the lack of nationalistic chauvinism in important sections of the German political elite. Aggressive nationalist policies in the Europe of the 1990s seem totally anachronistic. I am optimistic that German nationalism will not represent a threat to the rest of Europe in future. However, given the extreme fluidity of the political situation in central and eastern Europe, it would be rash to make firm predictions.

REFERENCES

BARBOUR, S and P STEVENSON. 1990. *Variation in German: a critical aproach to German sociolinguistics.* Cambridge: Cambridge University Press.

COULMAS, F. 1985. *Sprache und Staat.* Berlin: de Gruyter.

GRAUS, F 1985. Kontinuitaet und Diskontinuitaet des Bewusstseins nationaler Eigenstaendigkeit im Mittelalter. In: Ureland 1985.

HAARMANN, H. 1983. Kriterien der ethnischen Identikaet. *Language Problems and Language Planning,* 7,21-42.

HOBSBAWM, E. 1990. *Nations and Nationalism since 1780.* Cambridge: CAmbridge University Press.

INGLEHART, R and M WOODWARD. 1972. Language conflicts and the political community. In: P Giglioli (ed). 1972 *Language and Social Context.* Harmondsworth: Penguin.

KLUGE, F. 1967, 1989. *Etymologisches Woerterbuch der deutschen Sprache.* Berlin, New York: de Gruyter.

OESER E. 1985. Methodologische Bemerkungen zur interdiszip-linaeren Problematik der Ethno- und Glottogenese. In: Ureland 1985.

SMITH, AD. 1983. *Theories of nationalism.* New York: Holmes & Meier.

URELAND, PS (ed). 1985. *Entstehung von sprachen und Voelkern. Glotto- und ethnogenetische Aspekte europaeischer Sprachen.* Tuebingen: Niemeyer.

LANGUAGE AND IDENTITY: THE CASE OF THE GERMAN *AUSSIEDLER*

Charlotte Hoffmann
University of Salford

Introduction

In the absence of a fully satisfactory English equivalent, I shall use the German term *Aussiedler* to refer to those members of the Eastern European minorities who have decided to leave their native land and settle in Germany, which was the country of their ancestors. *Aussiedler* is used as a general word. Sometimes the more specific term *Spataussiedler* is used in German to refer to those who moved to Germany in recent years, in contrast with people who moved to the country in the post-war years of large-scale emigration.

My intention is two-fold: firstly, to explore the issue of national identity among German minorities in Eastern Europe against the backdrop of rapid decline in the number of German mother tongue speakers among these minority groups; and secondly, to examine the role of language in the perception of national identity among *Aussiedler* and among the receiving majority in Germany.

Tables 1 and 2 give an indication of the distribution of German speakers in different countries, and the decline in their numbers.

In the immediate post-war years, millions of German minority members left Eastern Europe and joined the waves of refugees who moved to West Germany. In the 1950s, emigration came to a virtual halt, and in the 1960s and 1970s, only relatively small numbers of *Aussiedler* arrived in Germany, between 20 and 40 thousand. The end of the 1980s saw an upsurge in emigration: in 1978 over 100,000 came, followed by some 200,000 in 1988 and over 375,000 in 1989. All in all, something like 2 million *Aussiedler* have arrived since 1960. The largest number, perhaps two thirds of the total, left from Poland; approximately one fifth was contributed by each of the Soviet Union and Romania.

From a sociolinguistic point of view, we are concerned here with a group of people who have no parallel in contemporary minority situations. They abandon their minority status not

Table 1: number of ethnic Germans in Eastern Europe.

1939	1960	1989
17,000,000	4,000,000	2,800,000

Table 2: number of ethnic German speakers in Eastern Europe

USSR	1979	1.1m people with German mother tongue
Poland	1983	1.1m German nationals, as per German law
Poland	1957	1.1m autochthonous people, according to the Polish view
Romania	1989	0.2m citizens with German nationality
Czechoslovakia	1980	0.06m citizens with German nationality
Hungary	1979	8-9 thousand German speakers

source: Deutschsprachige Minderheiten 1989

by joining the majority of the country in which they are resident, but by moving to another country altogether. By doing so, they reverse the process of language shift which had become typical of their communities. Studies of language shift usually end at the point where the shift from minority to majority language has been completed. In the case of the *Aussiedler* we can observe a third stage, that of recovery of the minority language, together with a readaptation to German values and culture.

Research into German minorities
Research into German minorities appears to have flourished in two distinct periods. In the 1920s and 30s, publications in this area were of a largely anthropological and folkloristic nature. After the second world war there was nothing until in the late 1970s, research activities in this area began to cover a variety of socio-political and socio-

cultural issues. More recently, Glasnost, and the end of the cold war have facilitated fieldwork among minorities. Even more importantly, the new political and cultural climate has brought about a change of the attitudes towards minorities in general, and German minorities in particular.

A recurring problem encountered by researchers in this area is the lack of reliable data. There is often a considerable discrepancy in the figures relating to ethnic Germans and mother tongue speakers quoted in different sources, and one is often forced to work with estimates rather than accurate figures. Some data can be found in reports and surveys authored by community organisations, minority representatives or local archives. Often the only data available comes from interviews with *Spätaussiedler*. On the whole, quantitative information supplied by national censuses is considered to be more reliable than data collected otherwise.

Whatever method of data collection is involved, however, one needs to bear in mind that there are different ways of designing questionnaires and phrasing questions, of suggesting answers, of evaluating them and of presenting the results. Questions on language are not always asked. But if they are, they may refer to "mother tongue" or to "home language", or even to "language of daily communication", without further explanation. Questions on the knowledge of particular languages can be of limited value, as they say little or nothing about the actual language use or the degree of linguistic competence. It often seems that people talk about their "mother tongue" in the sense of "first language learnt" or "the language of the minority with which they identify", without regard to their standard of proficiency in this language.

Questions on nationality present data that can be equally difficult to interpret. Sometimes there are no questions relating to nationality itself, although questions about citizenship or residential status may be included. The inclusion of a question on nationality in official censuses obviously reflects the state's policy towards minorities. Thus, Romania and the Soviet Union declare themsleves to be multi-ethnic and multinational, whereas Poland declared itself to be a one-nation state in 1951. Soviet censuses contain a question on nationality, in reply to which people can state which their nationality is, according to the national group to which they ascribe themselves. Parents decide for their children. At each census, each individual can decide anew on his or her nationality. However, the nationality entry in their identity cards remains unchanged.

At times of openly hostile policies towards ethnic
minorities, and the Germans in particular, many will have
preferred to conceal their national and linguistic affinities
for fear of possible consequences.

German minorities in Eastern Europe

From the 11th and 12th centuries onwards east and southeast
Europe received successive waves of German immigration.
German settlers came from many different social and
geographical backgrounds, and for a variety of reasons,
economic, political or religious. German settlement areas
varied in size and geographical homogeneity, in the degree of
their cultural and social cohesion, and in the extent of
cultural and political freedom that they enjoyed. They also
varied in the type of dialect used and the degree of contact
they maintained with spoken and written forms of Standard
High German. On the whole, until the beginning of the second
world war, when seventeen and a half million Germans were
living in Eastern Europe, most German minorities remained as
a distinct cultural group, although a certain amount of
assimilation had taken place. More often than not, these
people were bilingual or multilingual, as for most of them
German remained the language that they acquired first and
used as the home language. For many, German was also used in
the domains of work, the church and the school.

The numbers, as well as the fortunes, of German minorities
changed dramatically after 1945. The war and its aftermath
(emigration, expulsion and resettlement) took their toll.
Stalinist policies, generally hostile towards minorities,
meant a change in the legal and social position of minority
members. Suppression of all manifestations of cultural
identity, which often included the right to speak German in
public and to have their children educated in German schools,
began to weaken the position of the language, as new
generations of children grew up increasingly as monolingual
speakers in the majority language. The cohesion of the
settlement areas was broken up as forced, and often repeated,
resettlement displaced ethnic Germans from their traditional
areas. In the USSR, there was a shift of Germans from the
European part of the Union (Crimea, Ukraine, the Volga basin
and the Baltic republics), to the Asian parts of the Soviet
Union (the Kazakh, Kirgiz and Uzbek republics).

During the years of the cold war the German minorities were
in much the same position in the various east European
countries, although the specific degree of suppression or
intolerance that they suffered depended to some extent on
whether the respective state constitutions allowed meaningful

rights to nationalities. In fact, the reasons still adduced by *Aussiedler* for emigrating to West Germany give prominence to their desire to escape from harassment, the wish to be free to express their national identity and, in the case of compulsorily resettled Germans and their dependents, the feeling of rootlessness caused by the loss of their native land.

Today, there are an estimated three million ethnic Germans in Eastern Europe, half of them in the USSR, an quarter in Poland and the remainder in Hungary, Czechoslovakia and Romania. Emigration to Germany is still intense, and it results in large-scale abandonment of rural settlements. It is said that within one generation there will be no Germans left in Hungary, Czechoslovakia and Romania.

The position of German among ethnic Germans

If the number of ethnic Germans has fallen considerably during the last 50 years, this is even more true in the case of Mother Tongue speakers. In the USSR, approximately 50% of the Germans are listed as Mother Tongue speakers, but for many of them, German is very much a lesser-used language. In some countries - Hungary, Czechoslovakia, Romania and parts of Poland - the numbers are now so low that German is unlikely to exist as a native language by the end of the decade. (Interestingly, perhaps, it looks as though German as a foreign language is rapidly assuming the role that Russian used to occupy in the former communist states.)

In terms of language shift, this process has taken place at unusual speed, with the shift away from German ofen completed within two generations. The factors that have most significantly contributed to the loss of German can be summarised as follows:

a) prohibition of the use of German in public, and a ban on publishing anything in German;
b) closure of educational, cultural, religious and commercial institutions where German had been used in the past;
c) ban on the use of the language by teachers and by the clergy;
d) lack of contact with the "mother country", and with spoken and written forms of the standard variety;
e) an increase in mixed marriages, which became more common as the cohesion of the German communities was eroded;
f) encouragement of the use of the majority language from parents who did not want their children to be discriminated against on the grounds of ethnic background;
g) the age structure of mother tongue speakers;

h) continued exodus of Germans from many parts of eastern
Europe;

The ethnic cohesion of German minorities has been
considerably weakened by political and social developments
during the last 50 years. The continued drop in their numbers
will eventually threaten the viability of their social and
cultural institutions and, by implication, their language.

Ethnic identity among German minorities
Any discussion of ethnicity and nationality remains, in the
last resort, open-ended. Whereas categorization by others is
determined primarily by group markers such as race, religion
and customs, self-ascription to an ethnic or national group
is less straightforward. In his early treatment of the
subject, Edwards (1977) suggests that at a very simple level,
ethnicity can be thought of as a sense of group identity
deriving from real or perceived bonds created by objective
group markers. In a later definition (Edwards 1985), he says
that there is no need for the continuation over generations
of the same socialization or cultural patterns, as long as
the shared objective characteristics or subjective
contributions to the sense of groupness help to maintain
group boundaries, and as long as group attachments relate to
an observably real past. This broadening of the term can be
useful in the context of long-established minorities who have
undergone a certain degree of assimilation with other groups,
including a shift in the pattern of their language use.

Similarly, Weber-Kellerman (1981) makes the point that not
all characteristic features of ethnic groups have to be
present at all times. Social groups are subject to varying
types of dynamics at different times in their history, and
therefore distinct combinations of ethnic characteristics
emerge from generation to generation. So, "to be German" will
mean different things to different people at different times.

In his study of German minorites under Polish rule after
1945, Stoll (1989) outlines two models according to which
individuals are usually assigned to different national
groups or nationalities. The objective model takes into
account only observable, external features, such as common
descent, culture, customs, religion, place of residence, and
above all, language, which is considered to be the most
objective group marker. The subjective theory, on the other
hand, emphasizes the importance of the individual's own free
ascription to a group. These models show that neither descent
nor nationality can be seen as absolute categories, as people

may be assigned to different groups, depending on which of the two models are applied in determining their nationality.

Incidentally, German legislation on the subject of nationality (dating from 1913, 1939, 1949 - article 116 of the constitution - 1953 and 1955) follows a mixture of the two models, taking into account such criteria as descent, language, education and culture, and also an element of self-ascription. Looking at German minorities today, however, how can such criteria be applied? And how much importance do they carry in relation to other factors determining people's lives? In their study of Germans in the Soviet Union, Fleischauer and Pinkus (1986) approached the question of identity by looking at successive national censuses (1959-79) and collecting from them data that served as quantitative indicators of national identity. In particular, they considered the figures for nationality according to population censuses, mother tongue, and identity card. They found that figures for identity card descriptions remained relatively stable, while there was a continuous decrease in the numbers in the census, even though the population is increasing in absolute numbers. Since emigration was very low at that time, F&P concluded that many Germans had "disappeared" because they hid their nationality by registering themselves as Lithuanians, Ukrainians, etc., instead - i.e. preferring a geographical rather than an ethnic identification. They calculated that proportions of between 10 and 15% for the period 1959-1970, and of 5 to 10% in the 1970s were involved. They also comment on the drastic decline in German-speaking nationals: their numbers had dropped from 75% in 1959, to 57% in 1979, and about half of these possessed only a rudimentary knowledge of the language.

F&P did not come across any official surveys that could provide information on nationality according to subjective identification, but they observed "signs of an intellectual or emotional nature" among the German minorities - an interest in the historic past, a desire to maintain national customs and German folklore - and a sense of special identification with other members of their own nationality.

A more subjective approach was adopted by Hilkes (1989). Part of this project was concerned with ethnic identity among Germans in the USSR. The interviewees were *Aussiedler*, and most of them were classified as German on the basis of their passport nationality, their ethnic identification, and their parents' nationality. The following factors emerged as the most important ones for maintaining a sense of nationality among Germans in the Soviet Union.

a) Endogamy was widespread among *Aussiedler*, presumably to an even greater extent than usual among Germans in the USSR. Rejection of partners of certain nationalities, and preference for members of particular groups as friends and colleagues demonstrates awareness of ethnic boundaries, and probably a concern for future group cohesion. Certain cultural features - belonging to the Christian religion and having German as mother tongue- were considered decisive factors for endogamic behaviour.

b) German traditions and customs were valued highly and maintained even among those who did not speak the language; for examples certain celebrations (like Christmas and Easter) still continued for the sake of their cultural content, even though their religious significance had been lost.

c) Religion was still considered a valid marker of identity. Most of those interviewed ascribed themselves to a particular confession. Even if they neglected some everyday religious practices (such as reading the Bible, praying or attending church), other practices (such as baptisms, church weddings and funerals) were attributed special significance. The language of religious ceremonies was, in the main, German.

The general findings were that there were quite clear indicators of ethnic identity among members of this group. It is not surprising that this should be so. At least some clear indicators of ethnic identity should be expected among *Aussiedler*: if they had felt less German, it is unlikely that large numbers of them would have considered emigration to Germany at all.

Ethnic identity and the role of German
Among those interviewed for the Osteuropa Institut Project, German was considered to be an important component of their ethnic identity by almost 90% of the respondents. But although the majority claimed that German was their mother tongue, over half admitted that their knowledge of Russian was far superior to that of German, and that German was seldom the language of everyday communication, even with spouses and close friends. Very few of the respondents had any significant knowledge of written German or the oral varieties of Standard German (Kusterer 1990).

A previous study in the same series (Hilkes 1989) was concerned specifically with questions of language use and language competence in the Soviet Union. Hilkes points to the important role played by German dialects (rather than

Standard German) as group markers: of those interviwed, 89%
were German speakers, and for most of them, the dialect they
spoke was considered to be the mother tongue.

Considerable differences in language competence become
apparent if the age of the speaker is taken into accoount.
Virtually anyone born before the second world war knew
German. Of those born between 1936 and 1955, 15% did not
speak German, and among the youngest group interviewed, 38%
knew no German. Interestingly, the proportion of those who
had knowledge of Standard German remained relatively stable,
between 22% and 28%, probably representing that proportion of
the population who had been able to maintain contact with
written German and German education.

With respect to interpersonal communication, Hilkes'
findings again show close correlation between age and use of
German in certain domains and also among certain groups of
people. Although the use of German with children, friends and
spouses declines steadily in relation to age of speaker, the
drop for those born after 1945 is very marked indeed, and
among those born around 1965 virtually no-one spoke German to
their children, spouses or friends, and less than 40% used
German with their parents.

The rapid decline of German has not gone unnoticed or
uncommented on in the countries concerned. For years the
German-language media, where they existed, expressed a
concern for mother tongue maintenance, described the
difficulties caused by lack of resources and lack of contact
with "the motherland", and the absence of support from
educational insititutions or society at large. The point was
often made, for example, that mainstream society would derive
some benefit from ethnic German children's knowledge of
German.

The overall impression, then, is that while the number of
mother tongue speakers is declining and the language is less
used, German still enjoys relatively high esteem among many
minorities in Eastern Europe. It has assumed symbolic rather
than practical value however. On the other hand, it should be
remembered that in neither majority nor minority settings
does cultural or national identity represent anything that
the majority of people are particularly aware of as far as
their daily routines are concerned. Personal ambitions and
concerns tend to be the driving forces here. Feelings of
ethnic identity assume greater significance at times of
pressure or threat from outside.

Language may cease to be a significant group marker, and language loss certainly changes the cultural content of a minority group's identity. If, however, the language disappears altogether, the most effective bond holding the minority group together is gone.

Aussiedler in Germany

In a recent article in the German weekly *Die Zeit* (4th Nov 1988), Roland Phelps, himself a German from Romania reminds the West German readership that ethnic Germans think of Germany as their *Mutterland* but they also have a strong attachment to their *Heimat* ("fatherland"). For them, emigrating to Germany means the price they pay for maintaining their German identity is the loss of their fatherland. In less emotional terms, emigration can be seen as involving a change from minority to majority status. This shift happened relatively easily in the case of the first wave of *Aussiedler*, who came to the West after the war, as they were not noticeably different from majority Germans. In contrast, *Spataussiedler*, who came much later, are perceived as being quite different from their West German counterparts. Their social behaviour has been influenced by the social and political conditions from which they came. Their moral values, too, are considered as different: families are bigger and more close knit, religion plays a more prominent part in their lives, and they often adhere to traditional customs that they consider as truly German. Yet many of these traditions have long been abandoned by most members of the consumer society of West Germany. The greatest difference, however, concerns language.

Fluency among those who do speak German may range from very limited oral ability to full competence in both spoken and written German, but the former is much more frequent than the latter. In all cases, the *Aussiedler*'s spoken German will be marked by dialect features with which the West Germans are unfamiliar, as well as by linguistic features such as code-switches, borrowings and syntactic interferences, which are common characteristics of immigrant languages, but difficult for native Germans. In general, *Aussiedler* are often looked down upon for not speaking German "properly". Language, it seems, is of crucial importance for in-group identification. From the legal point of view, the *Aussiedler* are German nationals, and many of them identify themselves as Germans according to subjective, as well as objective criteria. But problems arise when (many) West Germans do not consider them to be fully-fledged members of their national group.

Two group identification factors appear to be interpreted differently by ethnic Germans and Germany's Germans. One is the ability to speak and write German, which for ethnic Germans has a value that is largely symbolic, whereas for Germans in general it is the natural means of communication at all levels. The second factor is descent or origin. Descent, for ethnic Germans is interpreted primarily in terms of lineage: in the view of Germany's Germans, it also carries strong geographical connotations. There may also be a number of psychological factors involved when Germans refuse to consider ethnic Germans as their countrymen, but it does seem that language is the most important factor in national group identification.

Conclusion
What is often forgotten by those involved is that in many cases a significant difference between majorities and minorities arises because the latter, precisely because they are minorities, are not in a position to identify with only one group. Ethnic Germans in the Soviet Union, for example, may be able to trace their ancestry back to their German forefathers, but their culture and their language will have been influenced by those of the majority, even if the degree of assimilation is otherwise slight. The German minorities are therefore "also German", as opposed to "exclusively German". It is the transition from the former to the latter that *Aussiedler* have to undergo by adjusting to new values, and above all, by acquiring native control of the German language.

REFERENCES

ALEXY, H. 1989. Rechtsfragen des Aussiedlerzuzugs. *Neue Juristische Wochenschrift* 45, 2850-2859.

EDWARDS, J. 1977. Ethnic identity and bilingual education. In: H Giles (ed). *Language, Ethnicity and Intergroup Relations*. London: Academic Press.

EDWARDS, J. 1985. *Language, Society and Identity*. Oxford: Basil Blackwell.

ENGEL-BRAUNSCHMIDT, A. 1988. Identitätsbildende Faktoren bei den Deutschen in der Sowjetunion seit Beginn der Perestrojka. *Osteuropa* 38, 915-930.

FLEISCHAUER, I & B PINKUS. 1986. *The Soviet Germans: Past and Present*. London: Hurst & Co.

HILKES, P. 1988. Unterricht in der Muttersprache bei den Deutschen in der Sowjetunion. *Osteuropa* 38, 931-949.

HILKES, P. 1989. Deutsche in der Sowjetunion: Sprachkompetenz und Sprachverhalten. *Arbeitsbericht* 10, Osteuropa-Institut Munchen.

Informationen zur politischen Bildung 222,1, 1989. Bundeszentrale fur politische Bildung. Bonn.

KUSTERER, K. 1990. Ethnische Indetität bei den Deutschen in der Sowjetunion. *Arbeitsbericht 13*, Osteuropa-Institut Munchen.

PHLEPS, P. 1988. Deutschsein - was heisst das? *Die Zeit* 45.

STOLL, C. 1989. Die Deutschen im polnischen Herrschaftsbereich nach 1945. *Eckartshriften* 98,2 Aufl. Wien, Osterreichische Landsmannschaft.

THORSTING, K. 1989. Problematic integration of resettlers and asylum-seekers. *Sozial-Report* 3. Bonn: Inter Nationes.

WEBER-KELLERMAN, I. 1981. Interethnische Aspekte des Zusammen- lebens. In: G Rhode (ed) *Tausend Jahre Nachbarschaft: Deutsche in Sudosteuropa*. Bruckmann, Munchen.

NATIONAL LANGUAGE SITUATIONS: SOME THEORETICAL SOCIO-LINGUISTIC ISSUES

A Pachev
University of London

Sociolinguistics has not often placed the labels of "theoretical" vs. "applied" on itself and so it may not seem obvious that the applied issues of national language situations are in any way distinct from the relevant theoretical ones. Perhaps they are not and, if not, so much the better, for the distinction between theory and application is, at best a blurred one which is frequently misperceived as linear, i.e., from theory to application. Linear models of this type do not apply to the development of sociolinguistics. For one thing, the beginning point of sociolinguistic work on language situations was not the development and honing of theory in and for itself. Quite the contrary; the sociolinguistics of language situations began with real problems of the various political and sociocultural entities. Many sociolinguists were concerned about educational issues that grew out of minority language or dialect functions in society. Others were concerned about human problems of power, equality and justice. Still others focused on general communication problems, whether or not these problems concerned social or linguistic minorities or society as a whole. And the larger issues of language planning were continuously present. As it turned out, the linear "theory to application" model had no real place in such concerns, partly because the relevant theories had not yet been developed (e.g. a theory that would account for sociolinguistic variability in society, or communicative comptence, not just linguistic competence), and partly because the overriding concern of sociolinguists lay in solving the social and communicative problems of the language situation rather than in perfecting their theoretical models. Replacing the old linear "theory to application" model was one which Roger Shuy represents as an iterative triangle (Shuy, 1984: 102). In our case, the apexes of this triangle are sociolinguistic problems, sociolinguistic theories, and applications of theories. Feedback between these apexes goes in both directions.

Commonly the real problems of language determine both the sociolinguistic theories usd for their conceptualisation or analysis and the applications of the theories. In cases where real human problems are involved, theory cannot be abstract or divorced from application. Adequate sociolinguistic engagement in real human problems requires the selection and development of both theory and application at least to minimise the number of cases in which theoretical constructs and their application create rather than solve social problems of language life.

One can argue that nowhere do the theoretical issues of the science of language and society emerge more strongly than in relation to questions of the sociolinguistic modelling of national language situations. It is very important to recognise how much national diversity can give rise to those issues. Just to give a general idea of the scope of the evidence that national diversity usually means diversity of language problems, contemporary political entities comprising a homogeneous ethnic group are almost non-existent. A study of the 132 states existing in 1971 found that only 12 were more or less monoethnic; 50 contained a major ethnic group comprising more than three quarters of the population; in 39 states, the largest ethnic group comprised less than half the population (Connor, 1978). Some ethnic groups span more than one community; the Lapps, for example are a transnational group that lives in Sweden, Norway, Finland and the Soviet Union, and the Jews of the Diaspora represent another social group that transcends any one country. Ethnic and state loyalties thus rarely coincide and when different languages are formally associated with these concepts the probability of language conflict is real, as can be seen in the many cases worldwide where separatist political demands are being nourished by linguistic nationalism.

Some of the most difficult endeavours of the sociolinguist are to try to define the bonds that motivate a language situation and to predict which elements of this situation will contribute most to its national character. Within sociolinguistics the conceptual basis for such a discussion has been controversial; which notions (e.g., ethnicity, nation, nationality, ethnic group, social class, cultural community, linguistic community) are most important. It has not always proved easy to work consistently within such notions, especially when cross-cultural comparisons are involved. Factors such as historical and cultural lineage, social status and cultural affinities often conflict or are defined with reference to differing criteria.

The description and explanation of national diversity in sociolinguistic terms produces complex questions to which there is no easy answer. The difficulties lie firstly in the variety of social problems of language life in different countries, which leads both to a variety of theoretical concepts or models and to different applications used for the latter. Secondly, there are difficulties with diffferent conceptual and methodological instrumentaria which sometimes provide different conceptualisations of nation-specific problems of language communication as well as for various strategies used in solving these problems. Thus progress can be made by recognising only the broadest distinctions such as level of linguistic relatedness or functional relations.

Such broad distinctions do have advantages in the construction of sociolinguistic models, or at least they seem to satisfy to a great degree the linguists' interest in language situations, presenting them with a comparatively detailed scale of more or less clearly and objectively defined components (e.g. language types can be classed as standard, classical, artificial, vernacular, dialect, creole pidgin) and language functions (e.g. official, nationalist, group, educational, wider communication, international, school subject, religious). All this makes it easier to describe a language in familiar terms and also allows us to work out a unified metalanguage for the systemic presentation of certain sociolinguistic patterns which tend to recur in different languages worldwide.

The clearest examples are probably the results from the efforts of the 1960s to discover general patterns in the sociolinguistics of language that would facilitate comparisons among countries. As we know, the efforts developed into two kinds of approach: typologies and formulas.

The typologies were attempts to set up categories based on a few variables into which any nation could be placed. They emphasised the historical development of nations, the legal status of various languages in countries, the relative position of the ruling nationality to the country as a whole, questions of language development and relatedness, and the size of the populations speaking various languages. See Kloss(1966, 1968), Rustow (1968) and Ferguson (1962, 1966).

The formulas contained language types and functions, allowed diglossia to be expressed and provided for indications of the size of the populations speaking different languages; see Stewart (1962,1968) and Ferguson (1966).

But although a great deal of thought was put into these typological schemes by scholars of considerable ability, none of them seems to have been widely and undisputedly accepted as the conventional method of representing societal multilingualism. Sometimes, it is argued that the failure of the formulaic aproaches marks a disappointing history for the area of sociolinguistic modelling of national language sitations. As we know, the profile formulas and typologies were required only to organise languages with respect to nations (or the reverse), and allow comparisons among nations. But clearly any number of possible sociolinguistic systems would provide reasonable organization and as long as the same system is used for all countries, comparison is possible as well. We have to agree that it is only when explanation and prediction are expected of the organizing principle that we can begin to speak meaningfully of right and wrong systems, and hope to find the right ones.

How did these formulaic approaches fail? To start with, some of the definitions used are not entirely clear. For example, on what grounds is the qualification "an official language of the country" given the same sociolinguistic status as "a language spoken as a native by more than 25% of the population or by more than one million people", provided a language qualifies as a "major language" if it meets the one or the other of the above qualifications? The official function itself has almost always been assigned to whatever languages have been declared official in the constitutions or laws of the countries, regardless of whether or not they actually perform that function. English was actually an official language of India before the 1967 law declared it so; Irish still is not much of a functioning official language in Ireland, in spite of being so designated in the Irish constitution. The language of education is another such function. The existing formulas will list languages as having the education function if the school policy is to use that language, regardless of whether or not teachers actually end up speaking some other language most of the time in the classroom, and regardless of whether or not much educating is really accomplished if the designated language is strictly used or adhered to. Very often the discrepancy between the legal status of a language and its actual status is by itself a social problem of concern in the linguistic communities.

The principles of explanation and prediction were not a basis for the formulas and typologies of the 1960s; instead the purpose was categorization and comparison. The new theoretical developments after the 1960s have proved more promising for the purpose of improving the explanatory and predictive adequacy of the sociolinguistic models of national language situations. Several successful efforts of the kind may be traced along the development of the concept of

"diglossia" from Ferguson's original proposal to an important
and general principle that seems to apply to a wide variety
of national language situations around the world (see
Ferguson 1972, Fishman 1972, Fasold 1984). The definition of
broad diglossia for example, which Fasold gives in his recent
book on sociolinguistics, is readily interpreted as a set of
the following predictions: - most societies have a verbal
repertoire that includes a substantial range of variation; -
some parts of this repertoire are more highly valued than
others by the community; - the lower-valued parts are
learned earlier and informally; -the higher valued ones are
learned later and more formally; - an important subset of the
language functions in a society can be ordered along a
continuum from formal and guarded to informal and relaxed; -
the more highly-valued segments of the community repertoire
will be used for the formal and guarded functions, and
vice-versa.

These predictions help to explain the superposed bilingualism
in Tanzania, Malaysia or India, the classic diglossia in
Greece, Haiti or the Arab countries and the style shifting in
Bulgarian, Russian or Hindi as subtypes of broad diglossia.

One does not need to be a sociolinguist to sense that
although some patterns of language life seem to recur
regardless of location or language, the national language
situation in the above countries features a great number of
significant sociolinguistic differences.

But one does need to be a sociolinguist to acknowledge that
broad diglossic systems of classification are unlikely to be
adequate to the task of explaining both the the
sociolinguistic similarities and differences within the vast
range of social and cultural patterns of those countries. For
one thing, by closer examination of the relevant
sociolinguistic data for those countries we could find out
that there is at least a strong tendency for a language
variety to be unique in its relative sociolcultural
evaluations within the community; for some speakers those
evaluations are closely associated with formality of social
interaction; for others the criterion is the social status of
speakers and for others it is the sex of speakers ... and so
on through a wide variety of combinations and permutations of
different socioclutural and sociopsychological influences.

If the only concepts we have for describing such facts are
"high" and "low" (prestige, variety or function), then we can
choose either to ignore the different socially meaningful
evaluations of the variety with in the community and assign

them all to the same category, or we can recognise the meaningful differences and distinguish the relevant attributes for capturing the hierarchy within the evaluative system of the community and its members. If we choose the latter option then we have to recognise that the evaluative criteria do not always (as Fasold's predictions seem to imply) match the functional ones. An example is the situation in Greece where the classic diglossia relationship between katharevusa and demotic Greek seems to have made speakers unsure of how to distribute their use of H and L, so that today there is considerable mixture of the two, especially in speech (Browning 1982). A "Dummy High" and or "Dummy Low" variety of language owes its significance in the community almost exclusively to the high or low regard in which people hold it. Mandarin, a major language of northern China, is a "Dummy High" variety for the English-educated Chinese in Malaysia as it is not used for any real communicative purpose (Platt 1977). The local dialects in some small Bulgarian towns are "Dummy Lows" for the well educated Bulgarians as those dialects are used for all sorts of communicative goals - even for writing poetry (Pachev 1987).

The notions "High" and "Low" seem to be a rather crude and unsatisfactory basis for characterising the intricate nature of national diversity in language functions and language attitudes. The use of "scaled" notions of the type "Low High" and "High Low" for modelling the double-nested diglossia in Khalapur, India, the double overlapping diglossia in Tanzania and the linear polyglossia in Malaysia makes a difference only in degree, not in kind (Fasold, 1984). The proposed models seem to share some of the shortcomings of their predecessors, the profile formulas.

Here it might be useful to point out why the broad diglossia typologies are only partially successful, and the sociolinguistic models of national language situations are largely successful.

Firstly, the organizing principle of most of the models seems to be too language-centred - i.e., the linguistic components and their relationships have been the very centre of most of these models. This principle has allowed us to capture a number of sociolinguistic regularities such as that in many cases the social phenomenon is the same, regardless of the nature of linguistic means to accomplish it - e.g., the universal tendency of people to reflect their perception of the intimacy or formality of the social interaction in their speech by means of subtle stylistic shifts within the same language, by switching between two distinct dialects or selecting a different language. But as we have already indicated, if we want to be able to explain more qualitative differences between linguistic situations defined at present as typologically similar, we shall have to develop the organizing principle itself. At least this principle should be extended to meet the challenges of such sociolinguistically relevant evidence that sometimes similar typological relations between the linguistic components of the national language situation are determined by quite different social and sociocultural factors.

Another argument in favour of relaxing the rigidity of the language-centred approach in modelling national language situations might be the difficulties the sociolinguist encounters when trying to match the multitude of socially conditioned differentiations in language and its use with the system of linguistic varieties or existential forms of language (standards, dialects, styles, registers, etc.) or when trying to differentiate among these varieties in a way that will reflect that diversity.

Secondly, most sociolinguistic models to date concentrate on the functional hierarchy of the linguistic components of the situations. By pursuing that goal a number of significant results have been achieved to the benefit of both theory and social practice. But the functional hierarchies themselves have been presented as a series of static categories, which seem to ignore the actual dynamics of the sociolinguistic processes within constantly changing sociocultural time and space. While the problem of "statics vs. dynamics" in modelling national language situations is clearly important, it is no less important to recognise that sociolinguistic typologies still do not take account of the relevant attributes which capture the social hierarchy of linguistic communities in society.

Finally, the state of the art in this field still lacks a well grounded and widely accepted sociolinguistic theory which allows for the balanced weighing of the micro- and macrosociolinguistic phenomena in society.

From what I have written so far one might think that I hold out no hopes of improving the current "explanatory" and "predictive" adequacy of the sociolinguistic models of national language situations. Over the past few years, trying not to succumb to such pessimism too soon, I have been working on a broad conceptual model of the national language situation, partly to ease the burden of the problems I have

already discussed, and partly to meet the demands for a
large-scale sociolinguistic investigation on the contemporary
language situation in my contry, Bulgaria. The result is a
short monograph (in press) in which I have tried to develop a
general theoretical model for the linguistic situation and to
verify some of its components on pieces of limited material
from Bulgarian in its social environment (Pachev, 1987).
The model (see Pachev 1987 for details), can usefully be
reduced to the following predictions.

-Sociolinguistic variability in almost all societies is
represented by the co-existence and interrelation of two
major types of sociolinguistic variables: - the broad
sociolinguistic variables and sociolinguistic variables
proper; three main sub-types - cognitive, interactional and
evaluative; each of these features language as both a product
of and an instrument in major social and sociocultural
behaviour patterns and important societal evaluative systems.
-The sociolinguistic variables proper represent the socially
and culturally conditioned variablility of language items or
units, functions, meanings and relations.
- In almost all communities these two types of
sociolinguistic variable show up in a whole range of social,
sociocultural and communicative manifestations. Two dominant
sociolinguistic systems emerge: the sociolinguistic structure
of society and its sociolinguistic communicative system.
-The sociolinguistic structure of a given society is
conditioned by the existence , functioning and relationship
between its three basic sub-structures (organisational,
functional and management).
- The sociolinguistic communicative system of society
features a substantial range of socially and culturally
determined factors. the overall variability of that
sociolinguistic system matches to a great degree the
variability of the structure of society and its components
within a given historical and sociocultural time and space.

It will only be as a result of further socio-linguistic
research that we will see and hopefully understand, the
intricacy of the relationship between the components of an
overall theoretic model of a language situation.

REFERENCES

BROWNING, R. 1982. Greek diglossia yesterday and today.
International Journal of the Sociology of Language, 35,
49-68.

CONNOR, W . 1978. A nation is a nation, is a state, is an ethnic group, is a .... *Ethnic and Racial Studies*, 1, 377-400.

FASOLD, R. 1984. *Language in Multicultural Classrooms*. London: Batsford Academic.

FERGUSON, C. 1962. The language factor in national development. *Anthropological Linguistics*, 4,1, 23-27.

FERGUSON, C. 1966. National sociolinguistic profile formulas. In: Bright, W. (ed), *Sociolinguistics*. The Hague: Mouton.

FERGUSON, C. 1972. Diglossia. In: P Giglioli (ed). *Language and Social Context*. Harmondsworth: Penguin Books.

FISHMAN, J. 1972. *Language and Nationalism: two integrative essays*. Rowley, Ma.: Newbury House.

KLOSS, H. 1966. Types of multilingual communities: a discussion of ten variables. *Sociological Inquiry*, 36, 133-145

PACHEV, A. 1986. Sociolingvistika. *Sociologicheski Problemi*, 3, 51-59.

PACHEV, A. 1987. *Savremennata ezikova situatsia u nas: sociolingvuistitchen podhod za neinoto prouchvane.* Sofia: Bulgarian Academy of Sciences. (in press).

PLATT, J. 1977. A model for polyglossia and multilingualism (with special reference to Singapore and Malaysia). *Language in Society*, 6,3, 361-378.

RUSTOW, D.. 1968. Language, modernization and nationhood. In Fishman, Ferguson and Das Gupta (eds) *Language Problems of Developing Nations*, 87-106. New York: John Wiley and Sons.

STEWART, W. 1962. An outline of linguistic typology for describing multilingualism. In: F Rice (ed). *Study of the Role of Second Languages in Asia, Africa and Latin America*. Washington, DC: Centre for Applied Linguistics.

STEWART, W. 1968. A sociolinguistic typology for describing national multilingualism. In: J Fishman (ed). *Readings in the sociology of language*. The Hague: Mouton.

LANGUAGE AND NATION: Africa

LANGUAGE USE AND LANGUAGE ATTITUDES: COMMUNICATING RURAL
DEVELOPMENT IN AFRICA

C Robinson
Summer Institute of Linguistics

Introduction
To the most casual observer of the African scene it is plain
that that continent is struggling with development - a
struggle that is perhaps most dramatically and persistently
played out in the rural areas. To the observer interested in
language and communication Africa is a rich multilingual
tapestry consisting of the fine threads of many language
communities overlaid with the heavier yarn of imported
idioms. Many researchers have observed the management of
these multilingual situations from the macro perspective of
national language planning. However, at the micro level of
the local rural language community, little attention has been
devoted to the effects of language choice on the nature and
direction of development intervention. Linguists (or
sociolinguists) have rarely addressed the domain of rural
development - exceptions are mostly to be found in the
developing countries themselves where research and
publishing resources are scarce (Bot Ba Njock 1981; Fluckiger
1984; Ohannessian and Ansre 1975; Pattanayak 1986; Tadadjeu
1989). Fasold (1990), for example, makes no reference to this
area amongst the possible applications of sociolinguistics.
Development strategists have addressed the language of their
communication only at the implementation stage (or not at
all) rather than as an issue in the design of projects
(Hamadache and Martin 1986; Robinson 1988).

This paper does not address the practical problem of language
development and standardisation which are essential
prerequisites for the use of the many hitherto unwritten
African languages in new domains of social life. Rather, it
considers more fundamental questions: what are the reasons
why African languages might be adopted for rural development
purposes, and what are the social implications of doing so?
The paper is based on research carried out in the Ombessa
area of S. Cameroon; the languages of the study are French,
the official language of this part of Cameroon, and Nugunu,
the local language spoken by circa 60,000 people (Stalder
1989), known as Begunu, of whom about three-quarters reside
in the Ombessa area, the rest in various towns of Cameroon.
Dieu and Renaud (1983) situate Nugunu in the Mbam sub-branch

of the Bantu branch of languages.

Rural development is a national priority in Cameroon where food self-sufficiency is a basic goal. This paper forms part of a larger study which examines the parameters of development intervention as well as sociolinguistic data, but here addresses in particular the relationship between language attitudes and language use in the community and how these influence language choice in communication for rural development purposes, which will be illustrated by reference to two examples of development meetings.

Language use in the community
Observation of language use in the community revealed different patterns in two different institutional contexts: those established by government initiative and/or under government control, and those established under other auspices. While the former are characterised by the overwhelming use of French, the latter demonstrate greater flexiblity and readiness to use the local language.

The dominant institution in terms of its influence on language use is the educational system which is entirely in French; Nugunu is used on occasions in the lower classes to furnish explanations to children at the start of their educational career. Nevertheless, even such limited use of the local language falls outside official guidelines. As children in the Ombessa area move up through school they begin to use French (as well as Nugunu) outside school. French represents the language of intellectual development, and schooling in French is seen by some as an instrument of cultural alienation. Since all development agents have been through this school system and acquired their knowledge and notions of development through French, it is not surprising, and hardly their fault if they assume that development intervention in rural areas uses French, whatever the role of that language in a given community.

French is also the language of government administration. Other African languages and interpretation are used when French is not known by all the parties involved. Occasional functions and ceremonies where the government administration is in control, such as the installation of a traditional village chief, also evidence the same predominance of French.

The one government institution where French is not predominantly the language of communication is the hospital, where systematic interpretation is used between the non-Nugunu-speaking doctor and his patients, and where nursing staff use the 4 or so languages of the hospital's catchment area as much as possible.

Institutions of the second type (established under auspices other than government) include the churches, markets, traditional courts and village development committees. The most important of these is the churches which rank just underneath government administration in terms of social influence. Use of the local language is the norm in church services; however, where the officiating minister is non-Gunu use is made of interpreters. In one Protestant church Bulu has been the church language in the past and survives in parts of the liturgy and in the songbook. The main weekly market in Ombessa is a multilingual occasion where native Nugunu speakers are joined by travelling traders and clients from farther afield; these use other African languages; French, Cameroonian Pidgin and Hausa are the main lingua francas. The traditional courts, both in the villages and at the canton level, are conducted in Nugunu, with the exception of written record-keeping for which notes are taken in French.

In general, situations might be grouped into four types of language use reflecting the degree to which Nugunu or French predominates:

wholly/mostly Nugunu situations: family life; also in the following contexts: young children out of school, customary court, village court hearing, main Catholic service, village chapel services, Catholic women's meeting, periodic markets.
multilingual situations (3 or more languages): Protestant service, women's festival church service, main weekly market.
mixed French/Nugunu situations: young men's football game, cocoa market, traffic at government administrator's and the Mayor's offices.
wholly/mostly French situations: schools, other government institutions, Catholic parish council, young people at main village crossroads, installation of chief.

At this point we need to ask how far this observed language use derives from and is reinforced by national language policy. Only two languages are mentioned in the constitution as official languages - French and English. There is no explicit policy towards the use of "national languages", that is the African languages spoken in Cameroon. While there is the expectation that all public business will be transacted in an official language, and the requirement to do so in fields such as administration, law and order, and education, there are no clear instructions for areas like development

services or adult education, though until recently government
initiatives in these areas have in fact used the official
languages. No obstacle has been put in the way of
institutions of other kinds to the use of local languages in
their programmes, though no encouragement has been given
either - until 1986. In that year Paul Biya (1986),
President of Cameroon, argued on grounds of culture and
identity that local languages should be developed and that
each Cameroonian should be rooted, through the mother tongue,
in their own culture of origin - this being complemented by
an accompnaying integration in the national community. Coming
from the country's president, this is an important statement.
It points to a a policy shift towards the use of local
languages, principally in the cultural domain, though less
obviously in official agencies. There is currently a certain
ambivalence in official attitudes towards the relationship
between the official and local languages: on the one hand
there is a recognition of the importance of local languages
as part of Cameroonian identity and heritage, but there is no
clear direction yet as to how such a recognition might be
implemented. Nevertheless, it is the agencies concerned with
rural developement that are making most effort in
understanding how local languages might be used in their
programme.

Self-reported language use
Villagers responded to questions on their ability to speak
and understand languages. The questionnaire addressed
self-reported ability and did not probe level of competence,
since this would have necessitated the use of different
methods and would have changed the focus of the enquiry.
Stalder's (1989) study of bilingualism in the Gunu community
serves as a point of reference.

Oral knowledge and patterns of language use were investigated. Table 1 lists the languages best known. In spite of
its status as an official language of the country, English in
this area is a school foreign language and is listed last.
Six people are monolingual in Nugunu, one person speaks only
Nugunu and Ewondo, and a further 17 people speak only Nugunu
and French; the remaining 55% of the sample speak more than 2
languages. The largest number of languages is understood by a
47-year-old woman who does not know French; the nine
languages she understands are Nugunu, Ewondo, Bulu, Eton,
Bafia, Sanaga, Pidgin, Basaa, Douala. Three people speak six
languages each: the woman already mentioned and two men aged
49 and 53 respectively. Age appears to be significant where
it correlates with level of education; thus of the 17 people
who speak only Nugunu and French there is no woman over 40

76

Table 1: Oral knowledge of languages among villagers

	% of villager sample	
	speaks	understands
Nugunu	100	100
French	80	80
Ewondo	15	57
Bulu	13	17
Eton	7	13
Bafia	26	44
Sanaga	11	30
Pidgin	13	19
Douala	2	7
Basaa	0	7
Fulfulde	2	4
Hausa	0	2
English	2	13

and only one man over 50. This would seem to indicate that the greater the access to education the less the need is felt to learn, actively or passively, other African languages, since the possibility is opened up to use French. Age, level of education and sex correlate in the group of 11 people who do not speak French: only 2 are men, aged 70+, while the rest are women of age 45 and over; all but one of these had no schooling at all.

Bafia and Sanaga are neighbouring languages and have been learnt through contact with those neighbouring groups, or in some cases because the spouse is from that group. Pidgin has been learnt either through residence in areas where it is the lingua franca (West Cameroon or Douala) or through contact with traders visiting the Ombessa area. Fulfulde and Hausa are also lingua francas in N. Cameroon and Nigeria and have been learnt, again, through residence or contact with traders.

Knowledge of English has been obtained through school, and in several cases respondents said their knowledge was minimal; one respondent said he had learnt it in popular residential quarters in town - this points rather in the direction of his having learnt Pidgin (which he called English), rather than standard English.

In addition to data on villagers' knowledge of languages, questions were asked on the patterns of everyday language use, in the family (with spouse and children) and in the fields. This last domain is significant for our study since so much development intervention targets the agricultural sector. The data for domestic use is summarised in table 2.

Table 2 use of language in the family domain
Figures show the % of respondents claiming to use a given pattern of interaction.

	respondent to family			family to respondent		
	Nugunu only	Nugunu and French	French only	Nugunu only	Nugunu and French	French only
Spouse	53	47	0	53	47	0
Children	51	49	0	46	54	0

Table 2 shows that there is considerable use of French in the home environment, though it gives no indication of whether such usage is manifested by the occasional French word or by whole conversations in French. Observation would seem to indicate that parents, with future performance in school in mind, want to encourage younger children to pick up French by using simple French instructions; with older children it may be more a question of the domain - school, for instance, might well be discussed in French, while health and food supply would be handled in Nugunu.

Whereas 49% of parents say they use both Nugunu and French with their children, 54% say that their children use both languages with them - indicating a perception that French is used slightly more by their children than by the villagers themselves. No respondent claimed to have abandoned the use of Nugunu in their home life. Nevertheless, the mixture of French with Nugunu does indicate the development of bilingualism, though not at this point of language shift, since parents are passing both languages on to their children Stalder (1989) using slightly different questions, found

that while a majority of respondents' parents spoke only
Nugunu to each other, the respondents themselves claimed in
fairly equal proportions to speak Nugunu or Nugunu/French to
their own children. He concludes:

> Looking at what language is spoken at home, it seems
> that Nugunu is spoken among the previous generation
> of the persons asked, whereas both, Nugunu and
> French, are spoken among the succeeding generation.
> (Stalder 1989 Appendix:10)

Data for the use of language in fields is summarised in Table
3. This domain is significant for our study since so much
development intervention targets the agricultural sector.

Table 3 use of language in fields
% respondents claiming to use a given interaction pattern

Nugunu only	Nugunu and French	French only
83	15	2

Field work is understood to be the cultivation of food crops
for the women and of cocoa for the men. Of the 17% using any
French in the fields only one is a woman. The expected
interlocutor in the fields would generally be someone like
the respondent, and this may account for the high 'Nugunu
only' figure in comparison with other domains. Nevertheless,
it is unlikely that it is only the nature of the interlocutor
which influences usage, since in the more intimate domain of
the family a higher proportion of the sample use French
alongside Nugunu. It may be that the domain of fieldwork is
felt to be the most traditional, the least touched by
modernity; physically removed from the outward signs of
modern life by virtue of the remoteness of most agricultural
fields, it is here that ancestral customs continue largely
unchanged. If this is the case then we may make two
observations:
- it is the cultural connotations of the domain of use which
influence language choice as much as communicative purpose;
- if Nugunu is associated with a traditional sector such as
agriculture, then one reason for the lack of effect of
agricultural development services may be the choice of

French in communicating with villagers.

In the light of the prominence of the reported use of French, we may ask whether the Gunu community can be characterised as bilingual and whether such bilingualism is tending towards language shift from Nugunu to French. While an impression of bilingualism amongst a significant proportion of the community is certainly given by the data presented on language use, an accurate picture must involve some assessment of the level of competence in French. For this we rely on Stalder (1989). On the basis of SLOPE tests (Bergman n.d.), Stalder found that tests of bilingualism in Gunu speakers shows that bilingualism in French is at a relatively low level" (p:481). This indicates that although the community widely uses some French, the level of competence would not warrant characterisation of the community as a whole as bilingual. This is not of course to say anything about the bilingualism of individuals, as Stalder points out.

These data on language use in the community and by individuals show that there is a high level of knowledge of French (80% of the sample), at least some use of French in almost 50% of households, and that there is significant knowledge of several other African languages, particularly passive knowledge. If knowledge of French were a major factor in the success of the development communication process then we would expect to find that process well-established and successful amongst a high proportion of the population in the Ombessa area. Data obtained on development show this not to be the case. We are therefore faced with various possible conclusions that need to be borne in mind when we turn later to look at language usage in observed development encounters:
1: the language of intervention has little or nothing to do with the success of development intervention; different reasons must be sought.
2: it is not the knowledge of a language, but the level of competence in it which is important.
3: it is not merely the communicative function of language, but also the cultural and affective functions of language which are important.

Language attitudes
Before investigating language attitudes as such, we note that certain attitudes are already evident in the data on self-reported use. The high numbers who declare themselves to be French speakers show not only a willingness to use French when required to do so, but an active desire to do so in intimate, and therefore less likely, domains such as the home. These covert attitudes may reflect a wish to be seen

as sophisticated and educated, whatever the actual level of use within families. Such covert attitudes bear out the contention that attitudes follow largely the functional distribution of languages; in this case self-reported use shows that local people give an important place to French, just as official public circles do. As we turn to the investigation of overt attitudes, the question is how far they reflect use and these covert attitudes.

If language attitudes are in the end attitudes to people, then investigation of attitudes towards Nugunu and French will yield information on how the villagers view themselves and their own culture, on the one hand, and, on the other, how they see the culture of officialdom mediated through French. If the aim of development is to enhance people's capacity to take charge of their own destiny, then attitudes to the way they see themselves within their own culture help in identifying how far development intervention is actually touching people's lives. If language attitudes are not taken into consideration by development intervention, we may expect a certain lack of harmony between what is actually happening and what development hopes for.

In Ombessa, French and Nugunu are in a kind of diglossic relationship, and we might expect such a relationship to be reflected in language attitudes. Fasold (1984) maintains that predictable patterns of attitudes emerge in such situations. As we investigate language attitudes we are concerned not only about how villagers feel about French and Nugunu (and the people who speak them), but also how appropriate each language is felt to be in the development domain. Saville-Troike (1989) points out that, in several studies of this nature, attitudes show a very high correlation with the functional distribution of languages. In Ombessa, where virtually all development communication is in French, and development agents have high socioeconomic status, attitudes to French in that function should be positive.

Attitudes were investigated directly by asking villagers to respond to statements about Nugunu and French and their use, and indirectly by carrying out tests using the matched guise technique. Seventeen atttitude statements were prepared in the local language and villagers were asked to respond on a three-point scale: *agree - don't know - don't agree*. In order to enable literate and non-literate villagers alike to participate in the survey, the statements were read one by one and oral responses recorded; comments were also noted.

The majority of villagers (62%) responded identically to the attitude statements - the 15 statements positive towards Nugunu met with agreement, and the two negative statements met with disagreement - indicating strongly positive attitudes to the language and its use. The highest number of negative and uncertain responses came from a non-native speaker of Nugunu, adding weight to the contention that people generally feel positive about their own language. Amongst the native speakers (all the rest) the highest number of negative responses was to 5 out of the 17 statements.

The most frequently disputed statements concerned the government's use of Nugunu. 12 villagers responded negatively to the suggestion that government workers should speak Nugunu. Of these, two remarked that there could be no obligation to learn it; one said those who knew it should use it; one was afraid of being spied on if they learnt Nugunu. Ten villagers responded negatively to the idea that the government should use Nugunu in written form; of these one felt that until the Begunu themselves were regularly writing the language, the government could not be expected to do so.

The word I have translated as "government" here actually covers a wider range of meaning than the English word and generally includes those involved in development services. Although the majority of villagers felt that these people should use Nugunu, a significant minority (23%) did not. This is an indication that for some language is not felt to be a prominent issue in interaction with development services, although it may play some role. Amongst the 9 villagers who made two or more negative responses to the attitude statements no particular charactistics or groupings of age, sex or status have as yet been identified.

While it is no surprise to find that villagers express positive attitudes as such, we note that these attitudes extend, for the majority of respondents, to the development of the language in written form and for development purposes.

Although there are some problems associated with the use of matched guise test in a rural African environment (Stalder 1989), we also used a matched guise technique, in addition to the questionnaire in an attempt to understand attitudes towards Nugunu and French, and their function in the domain of development communication.

Three versions of this technique were used successively in an attempt to obtain clear results. In all three cases the context of this test was a cocoa market which is the concern only of adult males, and so the sample was homogeneous - adult males (25-55) engaged in cocoa farming. The initial version followed the modification adopted by Cooper and Fishman (1984) with the aim of testing attitudes towards the appropriateness of Nugunu and French in the domain of development. The second and third versions moved closer to the traditional form of the technique with questions being asked, in the third version, on the speakers rather than on the content of the texts.

Administration of the tests was made difficult by the circumstances, notably the unfamiliarity of respondents with such surveys, the unpredictable level of literacy (which affected the way the data were recorded) and the uncertainty over the level of bilingualism of the respondents. In addition, repeated modification of the test meant that no one version could be administered to a sample greater than 22 people.

Results from all three tests do not present as strong a picture of language attitudes as the self-reported data, but do tend in the same direction, namely to more positive evaluation of Nugunu than of French. Version 1 showed no clear result - a slightly greater number of positive responses were given for the village text in Nugunu and the official text in French. For Version 2 the only fully negative responses to the text content were given for the French text. In version 3 no one ranked the French version of speaker X higher on any differential than the Nugunu version of the same speaker. While the size of the samples and the repeated modification do not give grounds for solid conclusions, nevertheless each test result showed attitudes towards Nugunu to be consistently more positive than those towards French.

Language attitudes do not parallel the distribution of languages in development functions. Group identity and feelings about the mother tongue exert a stronger influence on attitudes than functional distribution, even in the non-intimate and more formal domain of development. The villagers' attitudes are ambivalent. On one hand their self-reported language use evinces an acceptance of French, while on the other hand direct and indirect testing shows overwhelmingly more positive attitudes towards Nugunu, both in general and in development functions. Implementation of official language policy at local level through the institutional use of French exerts a heavy influence on language use in the community and this may account for the surprisingly extensive use of French in some personal and village contexts. A degree of conflict between use and attitudes emerges - the distribution of languages in the various social functions in a rural environment is not mirrored in overt attitudes towards the appropriateness of each language for that usage.

Languages in rural development communication
This ambivalence is nowhere more clear than in the domain of development. Strong opinions were expressed by villagers that agencies and agents, in encounters and meetings, should use/learn the local language. At the same time, development services were felt to be distant and removed from the real needs of the villager, even unavailable to them. Many factors enter into this situation - lack of resources (personnel), questions of training, or management, of planning, of distribution of power. Language is one factor alongside these - a significant one because language use reflects many of the other factors. French is associated with the official services, with government hierarchy, with education and a salaried job, with the urban-rural distinction, with access to power and resources. The local language is associated with village, farm, family, daily life, local relationships, and ancestral culture.

It is in the interaction between villagers and development agencies that language and development meet. The model of development intervention plays a large part in determining the language chosen for communicating that development, and, conversely, observed language use is an indicator of the local aims of development in practice, whatever the declared aims may be. Whatever the national development objectives may be in theory, on the ground, development services are more concerned with institutional survival and delivery (largely of advice) than with passing the initiative to local people.

The interplay between language and the model of development intervention is illustrated in two different kinds of development meeting which were observed in Cameroon where a significant, and perhaps the most obvious, difference was the language used for the meeting. One example of each type of meeting will be discussed here. I am hesitant to characterise these meetings as an identifiable type of communicative event since each meeting has unique features and cannot therefore easily be categorised. Nevertheless, in selecting features which are relevant to the dynamics of development intervention the components of communication offer a useful descriptive framework (Saville-Troike 1989).

The first kind consisted of meetings of the cocoa marketing

cooperative, government departments, and official training
sessions in the rural area which had been called and
organised by the government. Beside language choice, a number
of distinctive features indicated the official nature of the
meeting, and the top-down nature of the development
intervention, even where, as in the cooperative meeting, it
was said that the aim is to protect and promote the interests
of the peasants. A meeting of the regional cooperative
association was of this type and can be described as follows:

Purpose: called by the regional cooperative association to
discuss the problems and viability of the association.
Participants: 6 officials of agricultural and cooperative
services; about 40 local cooperative presidents and
secretaries - all men; one researcher.
Setting: a municipal hall with officials seated behind a
long table on a raised platform; others at some distance on
chairs in rows facing the table.
Agenda: 5 prepared speeches by officials; questions from the
floor, answers from the officials.
Content: Speech 1 by president of cooperative centres in
Ombessa - thanks to officials and reminder of cocoa tonnage
produced.
Speech 2 by president of regional cooperative
association - reminder of cooperative principles, catalogue
of current financial problems.
Speech 3 by president of Ombessa section of the political
party - exhortation to farmers to take the cooperative
seriously.
Speech 4 by regional agricultural official - exhortation to
farmers to promote the well-being of the cooperative. Those
who criticise must put their own house in order.
Questions: five areas were covered in the questions and
discussion - three concerned the functioning of cocoa
markets, two concerned the sharp practices of officials at
cocoa markets. Responses from officials included reference to
official texts (which brook no further discussion),
declaration of the limits of regional officials who can do no
more than pass complaints up the hierarchy, encouragement to
the farmer to prevent the initiative in cocoa markets from
passing to the exporters (who buy the crop), and one instance
of the question being turned around to accuse the farmer of
malpractice. During the questioning mutterings amongst the
audience on the hypocrisy of the offical responses reached
the ears of the researcher.
Interaction: at one point in the meeting a farmer was
threatened with ejection if he did not stop talking with his
neighbours about a question he had asked; this came close to
intimidation. His question was why the officials had not

apologised for arriving two-and-a-half hours late, thus
holding up the beginning of the meeting.
Channel: the whole meeting was in French.

It is clear that the speeches and the question/answer
session were under the control of the officials and that they
were at pains not to let this control slip away. Unwelcome
comments and questions were silenced or brushed aside;
genuine concerns of the farmers were evaded by reference to
legal texts and higher authorities. The official nature of
the meeting was evident and was reflected in the exclusive
use of the official language - in fact, only village
cooperative presidents, among the most highly educated
villagers, were invited to the meeting. In such a meeting it
is the distribution of power and its maintenance which are in
focus, particularly the representation of the hierarchical
relationship between the cooperative officials and the
members of local cooperatives. Use of the official
language is an indicator of this relationship, but at the
same time it reinforces it, since the officials are more
competent in French than the farmers, and they can refer
without fear of question to legal texts written in French.
Language use cannot be separated from other factors: like the
nature of the agenda, the seating arrangements and the
exercise of control, use of French is part and parcel of the
dynamics of power in this situation; use of any other
language in such circumstances would have changed this
dynamic.

The second kind of meeting consisted of village development
committee meetings, called and organised by the villagers
themselves for the purpose of discussing the development
needs and possibilities of their own village, and aiming to
mobilise village resources to that end. Use of the local
language in all interaction showed that the purpose here was
to involve everybody, to come to a common consensus about
the way ahead, and to ensure that every point of view was
heard. The distinctive features of this type of meeting
indicated the participatory and bottom-up kind of
development. A meeting of the Hiola village development
committee serves as an example:

Purpose: Regular meeting of village development committee;
discussion of village problems.
Participants: committee bureau of president, chief,
secretary, 2 elders; 5 men, 18 women, 3 children; 2 guests
(director of local CD centre - CEAC; researcher).
Setting: a village chapel building with bureau and guests
seated at the front; men and women left and right in front of

bureau on benches.

Agenda: Evaluation of recent set-up expenses and ceremony; road improvement; electricity supply; other business.

Content: Evaluation of the committee's installation by the local administrator centred on the reception the village had provided; general satisfaction was expressed, with the reservation that the meal provided should have been more European, since the administrator is an educated man!

The elderly woman president of the local communal field working group reported on their activities.

A report was given on the road and electricity projects with questions and discussion of possible sources of funds.

Other matters were raised and, if possible, dealt with on the spot: money was given for the committee's stationery needs; the woman president volunteered to find a yam storage place.

Interaction: The women were not only more numerous, but took more part in the discussion than the men. The CEAC director, far from seeking control as an official, let discussion run on and listened to what the villagers had to say; he took part on an equal basis with everyone else. Everyone was free to bring up items for discussion, and attention was given to each topic. The president was an educated man but born in that village - his position was respected, but his influence little greater than that of the village chief or other elders.

Channel: The dynamics of the meeting were reflected in language use; the meeting was entirely in Nugunu. The CEAC director (and the researcher at certain times) were dependent on summaries in French. The local people, whatever their educational level, could and did participate in the discussion. The use of the local language enabled control of the agenda and of discussion to remain with the the meeting as a whole - no one person could exert control. Rather than being in a position of power, the local official was at a disadvantage - a position he accepted because he wanted to see local people develop their own initiative.

Once again, the language chosen was both an indicator of the power relationships which prevailed, and it reinforced, in this case, the participatory nature of the meeting. These relationships of equal respect amongst participants are based on the fact that all were members of the same village community, whose normal, everyday means of expression is Nugunu. The committee and its activities are an expression of village solidarity and initiative - no official stimulus or control is involved. Although language choice can in no way be regarded as a cause of the "bottom-up" type of development embodied in such a meeting, its central importance is obvious

Table 4 features characterising meetings

official meetings	village meetings
eg. regional cooperative	eg village development cttee
called by administration	organised by villagers
offical agenda	open discussion
officials in control	villagers in control
prepared speeches by officials	few prepared speeches
fixed duration	flexible duration
official language	local language
attendance of elite	anyone can attend
under-representation of women	women present

if the opposite scenario is envisaged, namely the use of French in such circumstances. Immediately, some participants are marginalised (e.g. the woman president) and the power relationships change. Evidently the role of the official present was rather that of a guest than of an official as such; he became not a controlling influence, but a resource person to be called upon and drawn into the debate as necessary and desired. This stance contrasts totally with the relationship of officials and villagers in the regional cooperative meeting described earlier.

Space does not permit other examples of each kind of meeting. Even though such distinctions have been observed on other occasions, this is not to claim that all development meetings can be placed into one of two categories. Rather, these meetings are characterised by a bundle of features, including language use, which demonstrate widely differing relationships in development intervention between villagers and representatives of various agencies. These features are summarised in table 4.

Conclusion

The main conclusions suggested by the study of language attitudes and language use may now be summarised. We cannot reject the view that language is irrelevant to the success of development intervention, particularly where intervention has participatory goals, nor can we assign to language a unique or pivotal role in such success. As an indicator of social relationships, language accompanies other manifestations of such relationships. Level of competence clearly is important in that use of French excludes those with a low level of

88

competence. Cultural and affective functions of language are central insofar as language indicates and defines the nature of the relationship between villager and development intervention. Use of French evokes an unequal power dimension, manifested by a hierarchical relationship of officialdom to the villager. Use of the local language puts all the participants in communication on an equal footing, both in terms of ability to express themselves and in terms of relative influence.

Individual and community language use is constrained by heavy institutional pressures in favour of the official language, and this is reflected in what villagers say about their own use of French. However, the self-declared attitudes of local people point in the other direction - towards the development of the use of the local languages in development-related domains. This would in itself suggest giving the local language a place in development communication which aims to address real local needs. However, choosing the local language rather than the official language for rural development intervention in Cameroon will not turn the situation around so that the villagers' access to and use of services improves dramatically. Language is only one factor among other sociopolitical and economic phenomena which define the development intervention process. Nevertheless, it is clear that where the local language is used for such purposes, locally based development, the use of local resources, and the participation of local people become a possibility. Analysis of two development meetings shows clearly that language is an important factor which both reflects and reinforces the prevailing relationships of power and control and is an indicator, whatever is actually stated, of the nature and aim of development intervention.

The main factor in determining the use of the official or local language in development communication is the preservation of official status and the power which that confers. Changing from the official to the local language challenges existing structural relationships between intervention services and villagers, thus opening the way for a more thorough-going implementation of national polices emphasising self-reliance and village-level mobilisation.

REFERENCES

BERGMAN, TG (ed). no date. *Survey Reference Manual*. Dallas: Summer Institute of Linguistics.

BIYA, P. 1986. *Pour le liberalisme communautaire.* Lausanne/Paris: Pierre-Marcel Favre/ABC.

BOT BA NJOCK, II-M. 1981. Maîtrise des langues nationales et maîtrise du développement. *Revue Science et Technique* 1,3, 83-92.

DIEU, M and P RENAUD (eds). 1983. Situation linguistique en Afrique centrale. Inventaire préliminaire: le Cameroun. Paris/Yaounde: ACCT/CERDOTOLA/DGRST.

FASOLD, R. 1990. *The Sociolinguistics of Language.* Oxford: Basil Blackwell.

FISHMAN, JA. 1984. Language Modernisation and Planning in Comparison with Other Types of National Moderisation and Planning. In: C KENNEDY (ed). *Language Planning and Language Education.* London: George Allen and Unwin.

FLUCKIGER, C. Langues nationales et développement communautaire au Cameroun. *Revue Science et Technique (Serie Sciences Humaines)* 2,3/4, 7-19.

HAMADACHE, A and D MARTIN 1986. *Theory and practice of literacy work: policies, strategies and examples.* Paris/Ottawa: UNESCO/CODE.

OHANNESSIAN, S and G ANSRE 1975. Some reflections on the uses of sociolinguistically oriented language surveys. In: S Ohannessian, CA Ferguson and EC Polome (Eds). 1975. Language Surveys in Developing Nations. Arlington: Center for Applied Linguistics.

PATTANAYAK, DP. 1986. Educational Use of the Mother Tongue In: B Spolsky (ed). *Language and education in multilingual settings.* Clevedon: Multilingual Matters. 1986.

ROBINSON, CDW. 1988. Development Intervention in a Multilingual Environment: Matters Arising. Unpublished MA thesis. University of Reading. 1988.

SAVILLE-TROIKE, M. 1989. *The ethnography of communication.* 2nd. edition. Oxford: Basil Blackwell.

STALDER, J. 1989. An assessment of bilingualism in the Gunu community. In: *Papers from the International Language Assessment Conference 1989.* Summer Institute of Linguistics

TADADJEU, M. 1989. Voie Africaine: esquisse du communautarisme africain. Yaounde: Club OUA.

CHOOSING AN INDIGENOUS OFFICIAL LANGUAGE FOR NIGERIA

Charles C Mann
University of Ilorin, Nigeria

Introduction

The question what language a multi-ethnic, multilingual new nation should adopt has become one of the classic problems facing most developing nations. Nigeria is no exception to this generalisation. Nigeria became independent in 1960, and like most new African nations has been forced to grapple with multiethnicity, acute multilingualism, illiteracy, political instability, economic underdevelopment and mass poverty.

Nigeria has a population of about 120 million people, spread among 200 or so ethnic groups, who use about the same number of languages and dialects. One out of every five Africans is a Nigerian: the "Giant of Africa" boasts the greatest concentration of Black people in the world. Because of this, linguistic decisions made in Nigeria are not only of national importance.

Discussion about what language should be used for official purposes in Nigeria is usually avoided because of ethnic tensions. Among the Nigerian urban elite, the widely held view is that there is no reason to change the status quo. English is currently the official language, and there is no reason to raise one or more of the indigenous languages to similar status. While there is no immediate threat to English, there are good grounds for re-examining the socio-linguistic profile, and preparing possible alternatives to the present state of affairs. These ideas will be examined in detail in the next section. Suffice it to say for the moment, that the position of English as official language in Nigeria is not necessarily a fait accompli.

This paper will review the current language situation in Nigeria, the history and state of language planning, and enumerate the procedures to be followed if language policies are to be modified or the present arrangement maintained. Language is a resource of the nation. Its use in education, internal mass communication, and international communication needs to be planned and well-managed for its benefits to be fully realised. This requires a well-articulated and continually re-evaluated policy of language resource management.

Some clarifications are necessary before we go further. Firstly, the domain of this paper, language planning, should be understood as "deliberate language change...changes in the systems of language code or speaking that are planned by organisations that are established for such purposes or given a mandate to fulfill such purposes" (Rubin and Jernudd 1971:xvi), and "the organised pursuit of solutions to language problems, typically at the national level" (Fishman 1974:210). Secondly, it is important to clear up the distinction between an "official language" and a "national language". A "national language" is an indigenous language whose status has been raised to the national level so as to allow its speakers direct access to and participation in specific national domains - education, legislation, administration, etc. Usually, a "national language" is not recognised as a language of world communication. An "official language", on the other hand is a language formally selected at the national level for all aspects of officialdom, and would normally take precedence over a national language in any formal context. An "official language" is, often, a language of world communication. However, there are some cases where more than one language enjoys the status of official language. In the context of Nigeria, Hausa, Ibo and Yoruba are regarded as national languages, while English is regarded as the sole official language.

The language situation in Nigeria

Nigeria can most appropriately be regarded as a multinational exoglossic state, and should be categorised under Group C of Fishman's (1968) classification, i.e., a state made up of diverse nations in the process of forging a nationality by emphasising political-operational integration. Nigeria's indigenous languages fall into two groups: Niger-Congo in the south, and Tchado-Semitic and Sudanic in the north.

Apart from English, Hausa, Ibo and Yoruba are considered the three major indigenous languages of Nigeria. These languages enjoy national language status - the 1979 Federal Constitution recognised their use in the national legislative assemblies - while all other languages are regarded as minor languages. Hausa, Ibo and Yoruba would not qualify as major languages if Ferguson's (1966) criteria for national language profile formulae are strictly applied. It is more likely that they have been elevated to this status in recognition of the "Great Traditions" they represent, in recognition of the numbers of people who speak them, and as a hesitant move in the direction of greater cultural authenticity.

Hausa is spoken predominantly in what is still sometimes referred to as "Northern Nigeria". The dialect of Kano, a historical and commercial centre, serves as its standard. Hausa is a regional lingua franca, and is spoken by millions of other Northern tribespeople (Fulani, Kanuri, Tuareg, Nupe, Tiv, etc) as a second language. Before and immediately after independence, it was used as the official language of the Northern Region.

Yoruba is spoken natively by an estimated 20 million people in the south-western and western parts of the country. The Oyo dialect has been adopted as its standard. Yoruba can also be regarded as a regional lingua franca in so far as it is acquired as a second langugae by other minority tribes living close by - Ijaws, Edos, Igbiras, etc.

Ibo is spoken principally in the south-eastern part of Nigeria, and the Owerri dialect is its reference. It cannot be regarded as a regional lingua franca in the same way that Hausa and Yoruba are.

The principal minor languages of Nigeria are: Fulfulde, Kanuri, Tiv, Nupe, Igala, Idoma (in the North); Edo, Efik, Ijaw, Itshekiri (in the South). The fears of these minorities, who believe that they are victims of a vague policy of internal imperialism contrived by the majority tribes, are probably best expressed by Chief Anthony Enahoro (Schwarz, 1965:41)

> As one who comes from a minority tribe, I deplore the continuing evidence in this country that people wish to impose their customs, their languages, and even more their way of life upon smaller tribes.

This outline of the language situation in Nigeria would not be complete without an examination of the position of English, Anglo-Nigerian pidgin and French. English is the official language of Nigeria. Its use and spread are continued in urban centres, where it is spoken as a second or third language. It is for this reason regarded as a national lingua franca. Its penetration is not deep; few Nigerians, even among the well-educated, speak good standard English. Probably less than 10% of the population speak it at all. English in Nigeria is best clasified as a language of special information (Ferguson 1966).

Anglo-Nigerian pidgin developed in the coastal and delta regions, where it has its most proficient speakers. Though not enjoying any formal recognition, it has become the most

93

used language of intertribal communication, nation-wide. Mainly used in urban centres, it certainly has more speakers than English.

The study of French in Nigerian schools is mainly due to the fact that all Nigeria's neighbours are francophone. French has little or no penetration in society, and has remained a subject of instruction for University students of Modern European Languages. French too is therefore a language of special information.

Pre- and post-independence language policies in Nigeria.
It is quite difficult to describe the formal interventions of past governments - be they colonial or Nigerian - in the domain of language usage in Nigeria as language policies in the true sense of the term. The formal procedures of (i) data collection, (ii) examination of options, (iii) decision making based on (i) and (ii), (iv) implementation of (iii), and (v) evaluation of (iv) have not always been assiduously and meticulously followed. It is for this reason, that we regard these formal interventions of Government in the use of language as *language regulation* rather than language planning.

1: pre-independence language regulation
It is common knowledge that British colonial policy, unlike the assimilationist policy of the French, was one of indirect rule. Colonized peoples were left to evolve in their traditional sociopolitical and cultural systems. The colonial government respected and used their traditional hierarchies as a means of reaching the people. The British did not aspire to remake Nigeria in their own image, but concentrated their efforts in the field of economic exploitation. Prator (1968:472) attributes this policy to "the Briton's great interest in or respect for cultures other than his own coupled with his tendency to keep people of other races or nationalities at arm's length and to the generally pragmatic nature of British colonial policy." it could also be interpreted, however, as the expression of a desire not to complicate a sometimes confusing exotic experience.

It was the Christians who were the pioneers of systematic research on the language resources of each ethnic community they found themselves in. Their attempts to codify these languages, can justly be regarded as the first language planning the colonies had ever known. The colonial government, at first indifferent, got progressively more interested in the activities of the missions. Grants-in-aid were disbursed to voluntary agency schools, and later

Education codes were promulgated to regulate the educational system:
In 1882, the 1st Education Ordinance for West Africa decreed the sole use of English in teaching.
In 1922, the Phelps-Stokes commission recommended the use of the tribal language for lower classes in primary education, and the language of the "European nation in control" in the upper classes.
The European language Examination scheme required all Europeans to be conversant with one or more local mother tongues.
1926 saw the establishment of the International institute of African Languages and Cultures.
In 1927, the memorandum of the Conference of Colonial Officers on problems pertaining to mother tongue education in Africa advised that the mother tongue should be the basis of instruction, at least for primary education.
1931 saw papers in African languages offered in the London Matricualtion examinations.

In spite of these developments, the attitude of successive British colonial governments in Nigeria is one of quasi-indifference and passivity, with very little intervention by government. By the time Nigeria reached independence, some Nigerian languages - Yoruba, Hausa, Ibo, Nupe, Efik and Igala - had been codifed, elaborated and given an orthography, mainly thanks to the efforts of the Christian missions. In the South, initial primary education was being conducted in the mother toungue, while English took over for the remainder of the educational programme. In the North, Hausa was used for primary education.

2: the post-independence period
Since independence, successive Federal Nigerian governments have shifted from a neutralist/conformist posture to a pacifist/authenticist one. In their attempt to handle with care the still fragile unity of the country, the use of English as the sole official language has been maintained in all Federal matters, in secondary and tertiary education, and in broadcasting and media. By 1964, the UNESCO Conference on the use of mother tongue for literacy indicated that "Nigeria ... had arrived at no stated policy." (Armstrong 1968:232). In 1969, the Nigerial National Curriculum Conference upheld the view that the Nigerian primary school child should be "well-grounded in his mother tongue" for purposes of basic education. (Adaralegbe 1969:214). Northern Nigeria, nonetheless, opted for a "straight for English" approach, in which English would be introduced into primary education right from the first years.

By 1967, the creation of 12 states within the Federation led to greater autonomy over language. For instance, the Rivers Readers Project (Williamson 1976), which carried out an extensive survey of the various mother tongues of the Rivers state, was one of the products of state autonomy in language regulation. The six-year primary school project of the Western State (Afoylan 1976) was another.

The Federal Education Policy of 1977 made it mandatory for every secondary school pupil to learn at least one of the major languages in the first three years; in the event that he already spoke one of them as a mother tongue, he was obliged to select one of the other two for study. The Federal Constitution of 1979 states:

> "The business of the National Assembly shall be conducted in English, and in Hausa, Ibo and Yoruba when adequate arrangements have been made therefore."

and

> "The business of a House of Assembly shall be conducted in English but the House may in addition to English conduct the business of the House in one or more languages spoken in the State as the House may by resolution approve".

The Federal Constitution indicates that vernaculars can be used in the Federal Houses, as long as there is provision of adequate arrangements. On the other hand, the State House of Assembly provision does not mention any particular vernacular, and leaves each legislature to take such a decision as it may deem fit.

Today, in the absence of civilian legislative assemblies, English remains the sole official language of Nigeria for administration, the medium of instruction for the greater part of education, and the first language of the media. The national languages, Hausa, Ibo and Yoruba, are used informally in administration - probably more so than English - in the states where they are preeminent. In states where none of these major languages predominates (e.g. in Bendel State), a number of minority languages are used for broadcasting. The Federal Radion Corporation (Benin) broadcasts in Edo, Urhobo, Ijaw, Isoko and Itshekiri.

The options so far
This section discusses the main proposals for language planning in Nigeria. While the offical language question is primary in this paper, I believe that the whole spectrum of language planning strategies might be more important in the long run.

Table 1: Sociolinguistic profiles of Nigeria's major language options

	ENG	ANP	HAU	YOR	IBC
primary education	+	−	+	+	+
secondary education	+	−	−	−	−
University	+	−	−	−	−
Science and Technology	+	−	−	−	−
taught in secondary school	+	−	+	+	+
taught in University	+	−	+	+	+
International lingua franca	+	+	+	+	+
National lingua franca	+	+	−	−	−
sub-regional lingua franca	+	+	+	−	−
standard orthography	+	−	+	+	+
linguistic research	+	−	−	−	−
established literature	+	−	+	+	+
cultural identity	−	−	+	+	+
national identity	−	+	−	−	−
social identity	−	+	−	−	−
social prestige	+	−	+	+	+
national media	+	+	+	+	+
foreign media	+	−	+	−	−
business/commerce	+	+	+	+	+
parliament	+	−	+	+	+
political campaigns	+	+	+	+	+
religious preaching	+	+	+	+	+
courts of justice	+	−	+	+	+
TOTAL SCORE:	20	9	17	15	15

Table 1 shows my own assessment of the sociolinguistic usage patterns of the main language options (see Mann forthcoming for further discussion, particularly concerning the high scoring of English and the low scores of ANP).

Hausa
The position of Hausa is strongly supported by demographic

and sociolinguistic facts. Hausas make up about 25% of the total population of Nigeria - 30 million speakers. Hausa serves as a lingua franca in the whole of the Nigerian North. Paden (1968:200) refers to it as the largest integral political unit in Africa". Extensive linguistic research on Hausa, and a large range of publications are available. Trans-border communication in Hausa is possible all along the West African Sahel belt. International radio stations broadcast in Hausa. Finally, Hausa is generally regarded as an easy language to learn. Of all the major languages of Nigeria, Hausa is the only one to enjoy this reputation. However, in spite of these positive factors, Hausa suffers a real ethnopolitical drawback: tribal tensions in Nigeria are still so high that it would be politically impossible to adopt Hausa as the one national government.

Wazobia

The word *wazobia* is an amalgam of the various words for *come* in Yoruba, Hausa and Ibo. In the *wazobia* option, Nigerian children would pick up minimal communicative skills in each of the three major languages. This option is a symbolic compromise solution, which appeases the major tribes, but ignores the minor ones. It is basically a sentimentalist solution, and fails to consider how an indigenous language can be extended to cope with the demands of the modern world. This option was intensively promoted in the early 1980s.

A variant of the *wazobia* solution in **official quadri-lingualism**, mooted by Ogundipeleslie, who suggests that the Nigerian child learn his mother tongue, one other major Nigerian language, English and then French. This option suffers from the same drawbacks as the *wazobia* option. Many Nigerian children grow up acquiring at least three languages with varying degrees of proficiency, and usually they have some contact with French at secondary school level. This makes them practically, though informally, quadrilingual. However, formalisation of this individual multilinguality is hardly the solution to the nation's language problems. It exposes the Nigerian child to four geopolitically significant languages, but does not necessarily provide mastery of any.

Swahili

Swahili, a hybrid regional lingua franca, has also been proposed by Nigerians with Panafricanist aspirations, notably Soyinka. They see this choice as taking the unifying potential of language beyond Nigerian borders, while dispensing with the language relics of the former European colonies. Swahili has the merit of being non-tribal, and, like Hausa, is considered easy to learn. There is a basic feeling, however, that Nigeria does not need to import any foreign language for her own national purposes.

Esperanto and Guosa
Like Esperanto, Guosa is an artifical language, an attempt by Peter Igbinokwe to construct an indigenous language for a united Nigeria, by borrowing elements and structures from both major and minor Nigerian languages. Esperanto, proposed by Farukuoye 1983, seems unsuitable because of its typological distance from the language families in Nigeria. Both Guosa and Esperanto possess a socio-historico-cultural void that cannot easily be filled, and makes it difficult for these codes to operate fully as languages, rather than as simple means of communication.

Anglo-Nigerian pidgin
Although often associated with Nigeria's colonial past, Anglo-Nigerian pidgin (ANP) was probably already in existence in the multilingual delta area before the coming of the Portuguese and the British. These two latter events represent two main stages of adlexification. The evidence strongly suggests that Anglo-Portuguese input to ANP is principally, if not solely, at the level of lexis. All other levels of language show clear signs of overwhelming input from indigenous languages.

While ANP still has to overcome the stigma of being "bastardised" or "broken" English, it is probably the language of widest interethnic communication in Nigeria today. It has more speakers than English, and it has the edge over Hausa in that it is a non-tribal language, easier to acquire over a larger range of ethnolingistic groupings. Like Bahasa Indonesia - a trade lingua franca adopted as official language in Indonesia - ANP "can unify without arousing hostility and can provide a natural response to the local environment and the multilingual context" (LePage 1964:79). Its most serious handicaps are its lack of prestige, and its lack of literary resources.

ANP is used for news broadcasts, record request programmes, drama and advertising on Federal radio and TV stations. It is also used for feature articles and poetry in the print media.

English
The advantages of English as a world language do not need to be rehearsed here. English serves as a national lingua franca in Nigeria, but its typological distance from the indigenous language structures and world views speak against it as a

permanent choice. There is also the problem that imposing a Western language clearly underlines how the imposition of a Western language creates social inequalities between social classes, and emphasises the urban/rural dichotomy.

Other views
A number of Nigerian academics have contributed to the national language language debate, though these ideas are not widely discussed outside academic circles. See Osaji (1979), Rufai (1982), Okonkwo (1975) and Shofunke (1986).

The way forward
It is obviously impossible in a multilingual state like Nigeria to satisfy the all demands of every ethnodialectal group, either at the state or at the national level. Choices have to be made at both these levels about language use.

My own view is that while English cannot realistically be replaced as official language in the near future, more vigorous efforts should be made to find an indigenous alternative for the long term. English should assume a role as Nigeria's first foreign language, with French as the second foreign language.

While it is important to stress the need for some degree of linguistic homogeneity for the purposes of national development, it is not necessary to commit linguistic genocide against the minority languages. The 1977 Federal Education policy compels people to lean one of the three major languages at Junior Secondary School level, and there is no gainsaying the fact that this amounts to coercion, and is a diversion. Since each student can choose among three languages (or two in the case of major language speakers), the linguistic quantities and choice patterns of the student's verbal repertoire would seem to be of secondary importance. All that is achieved is that students are forced to learn one more Nigerian tribal language, classified as "major". The policy is based on the fallacious assumption that the mere fact of converging the multilingual repertoire of citizens towards the major tribal languages is enough to guarantee greater national unity and understanding.

We need to recognise that there is a delicate balance between the *instrumental* and the *sentimental* use of language in a multilingual context. To some extent, this is already recognised in the media. In education, however, the situation is more complex, and considerable changes will need to be made if an indigenous official language replaced English as the official langauge of instruction. These changes would mainly concern the time accorded to English in the curriculum, but it would also be necessary to consider which vernacular to use for primary education (usually the child's mother tongue, though this might not always be the case), which vernacular might be used at secondary school level (not necessarily the one used in primary school), and whether English should be retained as the official langauge of instruction in higher education.

A National language Commission

Nigeria urgently needs to approach the national/official language question frankly and frontally by the establishment of an active National Language Commission, with branches, called language committees, at state and local government levels throughout the country. The primary objective of this body should be to serve as a databank on all language-related matters. It will advise the Federal and other governments, and relevant ministeries on language affairs. It will also promote the preservation and enrichment of Nigeria's language resources. The commission and its committees should be multidisciplinary, with members spanning all relevant professional fields. The present situation, where all language matters are left in the hands of departments of linguistics and Nigerian languages of the Universities is not satisfactory. The National Commission will also be expected to map out strategies for educational development through mother tongues, for broadcasting, and to promote publicity campaigns in the event of an indigenous official language being finally chosen. Its research interests should include monitoring the training of language teachers across the nation.

Conclusion

Broadly speaking, a new nation's attempts to resolve linguistic dilemmas fall into one of two kinds: a linguistically homogenizing approach or a linguistically pluralistic one. The hope for Nigeria is to plan for uniformity in the *instrumental* aspects of language, but for diversity in the *sentimental* aspects. The crucial point, however, is that there should be a well defined language plan, that is subject to regular evaluation and adjustments.

The final decision as to what language is used for what sociolinguistic functions in a society is a political one. The linguist's humble duty is to have been seen to have done the spadework that leads to more rational decisions, of wider social acceptance.

REFERENCES

ADARALEGBE, A (ed). 1969. *A philosophy for Nigerian education: proceedings of the Nigeria national curriculum conference*. Ibadan: Heinemann Educational Books.

AFOLAYAN, A. 1976. The six year primary project in Nigeria. In: A Bamgbose (ed) *Mother tongue education*. London: Hodder and Stoughton.

ARMSTRONG, RG. 1968. Language policies and and language practices in West Africa. In: Fishman et al 1968.

FARUKUOYE, H. 1983. In search of a common language for Nigeria, in search of a common language for Africa. Paper presented at the 4th annual conference of the Linguistic Association of Nigeria.

FERGUSON, C. 1966. National sociolinguistic profile formulas. In: W Bright (ed) *Sociolinguistics*. The Hague: Mouton.

FISHMAN, J. 1968. Some contrasts between linguistically homogeneous and linguistically heterogeneous polities. In: Fishman et al 1968.

FISHMAN, J (ed). 1974. *Advances in language planning*. The Hague: Mouton.

FISHMAN, J, C FERGUSON and J DAS GUPTA (eds). 1968. *Language problems of developing nations*. New York: John Wiley.

LEPAGE, RB. 1964. *The National Language Question: linguistic problems of newly independent states*. Oxford: Oxford University Press.

MANN, C. (forthcoming). The sociolinguistic status of Anglo-Nigerian pidgin: an overview.

OKONKWO, E. 1975. A functional-oriented model of initial language planning in sub-Saharan Africa. *Ohio State University Working Papers in Linguistics*.

OSAJI, E. 1977. Language imposition: sociological case study of the Hausa language in Nigeria. *African Languages* 3, 117-129.

PADEN, J. 1968. Language problems of national intetgration in Nigeria: the special position of Hausa. In: Fishman et al 1968.

PRATOR, C. 1968. The British heresy in TESL. In: Fishman et al. 1968.

RUBIN, J, and B JERNUDD (eds). 1971. *CAn language be planned?* East-West Center Press.

RUFAI, A. 1982. *The question of a national language for Nigeria*. Bayeroun.

SHOFUNKE, B. 1986. National language policy for democratic Nigeria: a radical option. paper presented at the 7th Conference of the Linguistic Association of Nigeria.

SCHWARZ, F Jnr. 1965. *Nigeria - the tribes, the nation or the race: the politics of Independence. Cambridge, Ma: MIT Press.*

THE NATIONAL CURRICULUM

MULTILINGUALISM IN BRITISH SCHOOLS: FUTURE POLICY DIRECTIONS

Rosamond Mitchell
University of Southampton

In this paper I shall first of all examine the evolution towards a formal, national "language education" policy which is taking place in England and Wales within the framework of the National Curriculum developments. I shall review the nature of the arguments being advanced to justify the variable treatment of different languages within the overall policy, compare British developments with policy evolution in some other English-dominant yet multilingual scoieties (Australia and New Zealand), and argue that in the long term, the liberal goals of equality of opportunity and social harmony will best be promoted by educational policies which recognise the rights not only of the individual child to learn through his/her full repertoire of languages, but also those of members of non-English speech communities to opt to use the school system to advance the social goal of community/heritage language maintenance.

National Curriculum policy developments

The development of the language dimension of the National Curriculum has been piecemeal, with entirely separate working parties for English, Welsh and modern foreign languages, defined as separate subjects, and no single group responsible for "language" overall (DES/WO June 1989, March 1990a; WO June 1989).

Within this framework the existing differential treatment of the various languages of multilingual Britain is being crystallised further. Language in the primary curriculum for England has been decisively redefined as English. Ignoring many recent, local initiatives to promote the all-sided development of bilingual children's language skills (documented for example in Bourne 1989), the final statutory version of the English curriculum document contains one single statutory sentence regarding other languages: Pupils should be encouraged to respect their own language(s) or dialect(s) and those of others" (DES/WO March 1990b, p25).

At secondary level in England, this policy continues, except that a number of community/heritage languages have been included among those which may be taught as "modern foreign languages" (Arabic, Bengali, Chinese, Greek, Gujurati, Modern

Hebrew, Hindi, Italian, Punjabi, Turkish, Urdu). However, examination of the uniform Levels of Attainment and Programmes of Study proposed for all languages in the Interim Report of the Modern Foreign Languages NC Working Party makes it clear that these are targeted primarily at beginners with no prior knowledge of the language in question, who are learning it as a foreign language (DES/WO, March 1990a, Chapters 3 and 4). They do not represent an appropriate educational challenge for pupils studying in school a language which they have already mastered for purposes of everyday communication.

Of all languages other than English currently used by living speech communities within the state, therefore, only the Celtic languages with their territorial and historical claims to be "indigenous" have been offered a secure place within the National Curriculum framework (but within their defined "historic" territories only). Welsh is here the big "success story", with a range of National Curriculum provision being made not only for those in Wales who positively want it, but compulsorily for all children attending school in Wales (WO 1989). Not only MUST Welsh be taught to all, but a range of differentiated Programmes of Study and Attainment Targets has been proposed, to suit children in Welsh medium schools as well as those learning the language from scratch as a subject, with variations even here for those starting at primary and secondary level.

Rationales for current policy initiatives
It is remarkable that the redefinition of "language" as "English" in official policy has taken place without the provision of any explicit rationale. The final English curriculum document is perfectly silent on the question. To find an extended argument in official documentation, it is necessary to refer back to the Swann Report of the mid 1980s (DES 1985). Here, the view is taken that any potential benefits from the institutionalisation of community languages in schools, other than as single subjects at secondary level, are outweighed by possible negative social consequences. In essence, the Swann committee argued that systematic in-school commmunity language provision, and in particular, the use of these languages as media of instruction, (except for the transitional purposes in the early years) could prove socially divisive, and contribute to the educational "ghettoism" of ethnic minorities. The desire of non-English-using speech communities to transmit community/heritage languages to their children was recognised, but seen as something which communities themselves must take

responsibility for, outside the framework of mainstream schooling.

The Swann Committee did, however, anxiously debate the question, and its report does rehearse, before it rejects, a series of arguments in favour of the institutionalisation of community/heritage languages in school. Here they quote a research review they themselves commissioned (Taylor and Hegarty,1985).

This list merits further examination here, as an authoritative summary of arguments which were typically advanced in the 1970s and 1980s in favour of bilingual/heritage language schooling, in English-dominant societies.

The first three paragraphs on the list focus on presumed psychological, social and educational benefits to the individual child. Personal cognitive development will proceed more smoothly, increased confidence and motivation will enhance general academic achievement and existing linguistic skills will be systematically developed.

The next three paragraphs focus on the local speech community from which the child originates. Use of the community/heritage language in school is seen as having symbolic value, enhancing the status of the language both among community members and others. It is seen as having practical value, contributing to the vitality of the speech community through language maintenance and also as contributing to cultural maintenance and transmission.

Lastly the maintenance of societal multilingualism is seen as important for the whole society, both culturally and economically.

It is instructive to compare this set of arguments (ultimately rejected wholesale by Swann) with the sole parallel to be found in the National Curriculum language documentation, a section in the Welsh consultative report entitled *The advantage of bilingualism* (WO 1989, p.6). In clear contrast to the initial focus of the previous list on the individual child and his/her claimed "needs", the Welsh list begins with the social/cultural argument that language maintenance/transmission is the responsibility of educators today on grounds of linguistic antiquity and present day vitality, as well as nationhood/territoriality.

In paragraphs 2.19 and 2.20, arguments are advanced which

have no close parallel in the former list. These refer to the wider society of Wales and make the claim that a person without Welsh cannot participate fully in its linguistic/cultural life; here the line of argument is closer to that implicit at least in the English NC documentation for Standard English itself. It is also argued in the final paragraph (2.24) that a knowledge of Welsh is vocationally advantageous.

Paragraphs 2.21 and 2.22 also make an argument absent from the Taylor and Hegarty list, that bilingualism lays a good foundation for a subsequent learning of yet other languages.

Finally, paragraph 2.33 addresses the personal development of the individual child, given priority by Taylor and Hegarty. The claims made are much more cautious, however. The main argument is that individual cognitive development, and children's mastery of English will not be adversely affected by bilingual Welsh/English schooling.

The differences between thse two lists may be explained by historical differences in the social prestige, and the degree of existing institutionalisation both in education and the wider society, of the "indigenous" language on the one hand, and the newer community/heritage languages of England on the other.

For the low status languages with limited institution-alisation, the prime emphasis has been placed on the individual child and his/her presumed "needs". Moreover, for this child, a key argument advanced is that the bilingual/heritage school experience will enhance achievment in terms of "mainstream" norms and goals (i.e., overall school success), as well as promoting a sense of identity and providing access to the culture and life of his/her local speech community. While the goal of language and cultural maintenance/transmission is mentioned, this is done tentatively by comparison. The relevant speech community is not territorially defined; there is no expectation that the wider society would adopt the minority language as a means of wider communication beyond the group.

For Welsh, in contrast, language maintenance arguments take pride of place. There is a clear territorial claim, so that within the borders of Wales it is seen as reasonable that all children study Welsh, not only those from currently Welsh-using communities. This is argued to be necessary for full participation in the public life of Wales. On the other hand, arguments about possible enhancement of individual children's cognitive and academic achievments are much less central to the Welsh case, and are advanced with considerable caution.

The arguments being currently advanced for bilingual education involving the new community/heritage languages are thus primarily educational; the arguments involving the "indigenous" language are primarily social and cultural.

Whatever the merits of the respective sets of arguments, however, it is clear that Welsh has done very substantially better out of the National Curiculum policy "settlement" than any other minority language.

This sympathetic treatment of Welsh may indeed not actually depend on the merits of the arguments explicitly advanced. Welsh has a long start over the community languages of England, with a revivalist movement dating from the 19th century and a concern with maintenace via the education system as a longstanding element within that movement. Its "territoriality" claims to have powerful roots in British history, and contemporary political structures. It has long had an articulate middle class, as well as many migrant "sympathisers" dispersed through wider British society. For all its distinctiveness, Welsh culture is recognisably "European" in character, and the Welsh are perceived to share their ethnic identity with the majority population of England.

Whether such differential treatment, and the affording of relative institutional security to "indegenous" languages while newer community languages are effectively suppressed, are appropriate to a British language education policy in the 1990s and beyond, will be returned to in the final section of this paper. As a source of alternative perspectives and solutions to similar educational dilemmas, I will first consider the current language education policies of two other English-dominant yet mulitlingual societies, Australia and New Zealand.

Multilingualism and language policy in Australia
Out of Australia's total population of c16 million, around 1.7 million have a first language other than English. For around 30,000 people only, this is an Aboriginal language, and for another 30,000, Kriol or Torres Straits Creole. The rest speak languages of recent immigration; Italian, Greek, German and Dutch have each over 100,000 speakers. While in recent years ESL provision has increased and become more professionalised, Australians in general have a poor record

as language learners, with 87% of English L1 speakers having acquired no other language.

In 1987 the Australian Commonwealth Department of Education published for consultation its so-called "National policy on Languages" (Lo Bianco, 1987), with educational policy a main concern. Dramatically differently from our own piecemeal development of policy, this comprehensive report attempts to synthesise plans and goals for the teaching of English (as L1 and as L2), of Aboriginal languages, of other community languages, and of foreign languages, together with consideration of "language awareness" work.

The report stresses access to Standard Australian English for all, plus a language other than English, with Chinese, Indonesian, Japanese, French, German, Italian, Greek, Arabic and Spanish to be systematically promoted nationally, though locally important languages may also fill this role.

A special standing for Aboriginal languages is recognised, firstly because of their character as a repository of indigenous historical and cultural traditions, yet endangered status and secondly because of the uniquely "disadvantaged" position of Aboriginal children in the education system. The role of the school in Aboriginal language maintenance is recognised through advocacy of community controlled bilingual programmes in traditional communities, the training of Aboriginal teachers, and specialist resourcing for literacy materials production, etc..

For other, non-indigenous community languages, the report's formal advocacy of bilingual teaching is noticeably more lukewarm; the main thrust appears to be to promote the teaching of such languages as school subjects (though it is envisaged that this could be to the advanced levels appropriate for L1 speakers), and for support of community language teaching efforts outside the mainstream school. However, bilingual and minority language immersion programmes are also envisaged where local community demand exists. Generally, the expressed willingness to commit Commonwealth resources to funding non-Aboriginal community language provision in mainstream schools goes far beyond the intended scale of British provision under the National Curriculum.

Multilingualism and language policy in New Zealand
The linguistic situation in New Zealand is also complex. English predominates among both the white (pakeha) population and among the 400,000 Maori, who presently constitute 12% of

the population (NZ Government, 1990). However, te reo Maori (recognised as the second official language of New Zealand), is still the first language of c50,000 older community members, and in the 1980s a language revival movement developed with great rapidity as part of a more general renewal of Maori cultural and political identity. In addition, New Zealand is home to c100,000 Pacific Islanders, mostly post-war settlers, who have so far maintained strong language loyalties to Samoan, Tongan, Cook Island, Maori, etc.. There are also small speech communities surviving from earlier migrations (e.g. Greek and Chinese), as well as recent refugee communities (e.g. Vietnamese).

New Zealand government has committed itself to a general policy of pakeha-Maori biculturalism, and in education has shown itself willing to fund significant initiatives in Maori language education. Most striking has been the preschool, kohanga-reo movement. This Maori-medium programme began with just four "language nests" in 1982 (Spolsky, 1989); by 1990 there were about 800 kohanga reo in existence. An expansion of bilingual primary schooling has followed, with around 9000 children currently following such programmes, and a small number of all-Maori schools are coming into being. These programmes are intended primarily for children of ethnic Maori affiliation, and are linked to local Maori communities and tribal structures; a 1970s enthusiasm for teaching te reo Maori to all New Zealanders has dwindled, to be replaced by efforts targeting the ethnic Maori community much more closely (Spolsky, 1990).

Maori revitalisation (and government acceptance of the responsibility for resourcing this) draws much of its inspiration from a territorial claim; the Maoris are the *tangata whenua*, the indigenous "people of the place". There is a recognition among whites that the long term harmonious development of New Zealand society as a Pacific nation depends on an accommodation with Maori culture and identity, and not on assimilation (Mulgan, 1989).

However, the New Zealand government has also shown itself willing to resource educational provision, at least at pre-school level, where minority langage communities lacking such territorial "legitimation" show willingness to take initiatives. Thus, Pacific Islands pre-school language nests have grown from 14 in 1987 to 150 plus in 1990 (Burgess, 1990).

New Zealand as yet lacks a formal language policy, though a commitment to fund the development of one was announced by the Minister of Education in August 1990. Yet the main lines of New Zealand thinking are clear, and involve the recognition of the rights of a variety of speech communities, both indigenous and "new settler", to use the state educational system to maintain and transmit heritage languages and cultures, as well as providing individual children with access to English and to "mainstream" educational opportunity.

A new way forward?

The profoundly unequal treatment of minority languages within the British National curriculum is far more likely to create resentment and tensions than the presumably intended social harmony. It ignores existing community aspirations (see DES 1985, Chapters 10-14 documenting Chinese, Cypriot, Italian, Ukrainian and Vietnamese concern) and conflicts even with current educational reality. As a striking contrast to the statutory programmes for English, for example, the National Curriculum Council Non-Statutory Guidance on the teaching of English reinstates many references to bilingual teaching and learning as everyday facts of contemporary good practice (NCC, 1990). As professional language educators we must continue to point this out and lend support to local speech communities pushing for school language policies which reflect local realities.

In the Pacific examples discussed above, there are some important lessons for us. We may regard it as a sign of increasing confidence, self-awareness and political maturity, when minority language communities within English-dominant societies begin to seek suport from the wider society for language maintenance and transmission. In Australia and New Zealand, this is linked to a concern for high educational achievement, according to mainstream norms. It carries no rejection of English as the language of wider communication and of public life. The "ghettoisation" feared by Swann does not appear an inevitable consequence of educational multilingualism.

There is no impelling social good, then, which prevents us from extending to our own "new settler" languages (to use New Zealand terminology) the same language maintenance claims on the educational system as those now afforded to Welsh or Scottish Gaelic. As linguists, we know that minority language maintenance within English-dominant society is hard even with school system support, and almost impossible without, and that to say to local groups (as the Swann report did) that their language maintenance efforts are to be respected but to be excluded from mainsteam schools, is inconsistent if not insincere. We also know that as relatively newly arrived minority language communities evolve and produce new generations, (and especially if significant language loss becomes apparent), expectations of state support for heritage language maintenance are likely to increase rather than diminish. Lastly, we know from international experience that community/heritage language programmes are likely to be sucessful in English-dominant society, where they are "volunteer" programmes, genuinely enjoying local parental and community support.

Conclusions

1. Emerging British policy is now strikingly out of step with practice in other countries with similar educational traditions. A new policy for language education in Britain is needed reflecting multilingual realities in an equitable manner, to replace the narrow traditional/nationalist policy which has emerged within the National Curriculum.

2. Within such a policy, we should now recognise a place for all languages with significant contemporary speech communities in the UK, as potential media of learning and/or as subjects. The time has come to harmonise the treatment of the"indigenous" Celtic languages, and the newer languages within the territory. The issue of equitable and consistent treatment of "indigenous" and "immigrant" languages is indeed now a democratic issue on a European scale (Extra, 1989; Reid, 1990).

3. In allocating resources to the heritage language schooling, priority should be given to the education of children from relevant minority language/cultural backgrounds. This will lead as in other countries to some degree of special provision such as bilingual streams, "magnet" schools, etc..

4. Where such provision is made, it must be in response to clear demonstrations of local parental support, making a positive and voluntary educational choice. Students' continuing rights to Standard English as well as to heritage languages support must be recognised (Brumfit, 1989; Spolsky, 1990).

REFERENCES

BOURNE, J. 1989. *Moving into the Mainstream.* Windsor: NFER

BRUMFIT, CJ. 1989. Towards a language policy for multilingual secondary schools. In J: Geach (ed). *Coherence in Diversity*. London: CILT.

BURGESS, F. 1990 Recent developments in Pacific Island language nests. Paper presented at conference *Living Languages in Aotearoa*, Wellington, New Zealand.

DEPARTMENT OF EDUCATION AND SCIENCE. 1985. *Education for All* (Swann Report). London:HMSO.

DEPARTMENT OF EDUCATION AND SCIENCE/WELSH OFFICE. 1989. *English for Ages 5 to 16* (Cox Report). London: DES.

DEPARTMENT OF EDUCATION AND SCIENCE/WELSH OFFICE. 1990a. *National Curriculum Modern Foreign Languages Working Group: Initial Advice*. Darlington: DES.

DEPARTMENT OF EDUCATION AND SCIENCE/WELSH OFFICE. 1990b. *English in the National Curriculum, no.2*. London: HMSO.

EXTRA, G. 1989. Ethnic minority languages versus Frisian in Dutch primary schools. *Journal of multilingual and multicultural development*, 10,1, 59-72.

LO BIANCO, J. 1987. *National policy on languages*. Canberra: Australian Government Publishing Service.

MULGAN, R. 1989. *Maori, Pakeha and Democracy*. Aukland: Oxford University Press.

NATIONAL CURRICULUM COUNCIL 1990. *English Non-statutory Guidance*. York: NCC.

REID, E. 1990. European languages, or languages in Europe? Paper presented at BAAL Annual Meeting, Swansea.

SPOLSKY, B. 1989. Maori bilingual education and language re-vitalisation. *Journal of Multilingual and Multicultural Development*, 10,2, 89-106.

SPOLSKY, B. 1990. Linguistic rights. Paper presented at conference *Living Languages in Aotearoa*. Wellington, New Zealand.

TAYLOR, M and S HEGARTY. 1985. *The best of both worlds?* Windsor: NFER-Nelson.

WELSH OFFICE 1989. *Welsh for ages 5 to 16*. Cardiff: Welsh Office Education Department.

ENGLISH AS A SECOND LANGUAGE IN THE NATIONAL CURRICULUM

C Leung and C Franson
Polytechnic of Central London

Introduction

In the past thirty years or so, many influential educationalists in the UK have consistently argued for the mainstreaming of ESL pupils, and against the removal of second language pupils from the mainstream classroom in order for them to be taught English separately. (For a full background account see Bullock 1975, Swann 1985, Cox 1989, and Calderdale 1985.)

There are two reasons for this. The first is explicit. It concerns the issues of equal opportunities. There are ideological arguments involved which fall outside the domain of this paper. Suffice it to say that we fully support this position because, inter alia, paticipating in the mainstream classroom provides genuine opportunities to acquire the target language in a contextualised language-rich environment which makes high levels of cognitive demand. The second reason is only partly articulated. It turns on the notion of language *acquisition* as opposed to language *learning* (cf Dulay, Burt and Krashen 1982. Krashen's work has underpinned a great deal of current practice, as any cursory glance at in-service training literature will bear out.)

The purpose of this paper is two-fold. We intend (a) to examine critically the domain theoretical assumptions of the current practice, and (b) to suggest new orientations in the light of more recent findings in second language acquisition and the newly introduced National Curriculum.

Comprehensible input: popularity and problems

Krashen makes an important distinction between *acquisition* and *learning*. Acquisition is in some sense like first language development, in that it is implicit and to a great extent subconscious. Acquisition involves the processing of input by the learner in an authentic second language communicative context. It is more important than learning. Learning is a conscious activity and is explicitly about the forms and rules of the target language. Learning through formal and explicitly focused input will not necessarily lead to acquisition of the second language. For second language learners, the main function of the second language classroom is to provide "intake for acquisition", "intake" being "input that is understood". It is this suggestion that seems to have been translated into current educational thinking on ESL pedagogy. Roughly speaking, the best place for an ESL learner to acquire the English language is in the mainstream classroom while doing mainstream subject work.

Krashen also states that progressive acquisition occurs when there is "I+1": when input is meaningful to the learner, "+1" is the extra bit that the learner acquires in context. For Krashen, the learner's ability to produce language is said to emerge naturally and intuitively, and no explicit teaching is required.

Learning is related to another of Krashen's arguments, namely, monitoring. Monitoring is the application of conscious, explicit knowledge about the language used by the speaker when producing language. Krashen's (1981) Monitor Model contends that conscious learning plays only a small part in second language performance. Our utterances are intiated by the acquired system but our conscious learning may then be used to alter the output of the acquired system. Monitoring may generally improve the accuracy levels of second language users, particularly in writing and in discrete item tests. The optimal monitor user is a learner who uses learned competence to supplement acquired competence (Krashen 1982).

Krashen's theory of second language acquisition has proved popular because it is readily understood and seems to fit many of the observable features of the second language learning process. Krashen's views have been taken to support a very powerful assumption: by putting the second language learner in the mainstream, we are satisfying the conditions necessary for acquisition. Second language support teachers have simply been inserted into the mainstream subject classroom to help second language learners make sense of the language used in the classroom and to turn some of it into comprehensible input. This interpretation is extremely attractive because it simplifies the complex process of teaching and learning. It also suggests an easy-to-use model of language communication which ignores what we know about pragmatics and discourse analysis and so on (Widdowson 1990).

Although this line of thinking has informed a great many teachers in the UK, Krashen in fact advocates language classes for the beginning learner when real life input is too complicated. He describes a four stage language teaching programme which includes general second langauge teaching, sheltered language teaching, partial mainstream, and then, finally, full integration of the ESL learner into the mainstream classroom (Krashen 1982, 1985). This is not surprising: what he proposes is a theory of second langauge acquisition in the context of a second language classroom. For that reason alone, one should be extremely careful of applying this theory in the mainstream subject classroom context.

While we accept the general education principles of mainstreaming, we feel that there are flaws in this particular interpretation of Krashen's ideas. Furthermore, there are a number of theoretical difficulties in Krashen's work in the first place. Some criticism of Krashen's work stems from his lack of linguistic precision. Although he claims that acquisition is to be identified with a language acquisition device (Krashen 1985), he has not clearly described this acquisition process, but simply asserts that it is implicit and natural. Krashen's views in general, and his views on Input in particular, have been widely discussed in the literature, notably by Gregg (1984), Sharwood-Smith (1986), White (1987) and Gass (1988), who all argue that the learner has an active role in deciding what to do with input and how it is treated. On this view, it is difficult to see how teachers can be sure that they are providing comprehensible input for their learners: fundamentally, Krashen's theory lacks a psycholinguistic basis.

We turn now to practical questions. The current interpretation of Krashen's position is not always helpful in the context of a mainstream subject classroom. For instance, the individual language teacher in the UK is often provided with no specific training or guidelines on how to make what a subject teacher says comprehensible (see Bourne 1989). Furthermore, there is a widely held view that a subject classroom is a context rich situation, and that it is the subject teacher's job to make subject input comprehensible. This general view has prevented detailed discussion and debate on second language pedagogy. In the last decade or so, a situation has arisen where second language support teachers have effectively stopped talking about language syllabuses, teaching method, or any atempt to measure acievement in a second language in any significant way. For instance, in a recent survey of ESL provision in England, we found 28 LEAs which stated that they had an official policy on ESL, but only 8 of these had guidelines on the way in-class second language work was to be done (Leung and Franson 1990).

A more up-to-date understanding
Current research differs from Krashen on three main points.

a: There is now strong evidence that comprehensible input does not necessarily lead to acquisition (Hyltenstam 1985, White 1987, Gass 1988 and Swain 1988). As teachers, we know from experience that some learners do not progress beyond a particular level of proficiency in the target language, and fossilization sets in. There are a number of reasons for this. Firstly, not all second language learners are equally motivated to acquire native-like language norms. Secondly, locating a second language learner in the second language medium classroom does not automatically lead to acquisition. While learners may be able to make sense of what is being said to them in context, they may not be able to produce the requisite language without additional guidance and language using opportunities. Thirdly, empirically we know very little about how input, even if comprehensible, is treated by language learners, and it is probably unsafe to assume that there is a one-to-one correspondence between an instance of comprehensible input and an instance of acquisition. Indeed, it would be safer to treat the two as merely developmentally connected processes until and unless we find evidence to the contrary.

b: Second language word order acquisition research seems to suggest that there is an inviolate acquisition sequence, irrespective of the context of learning (Pienemann 1985). There is also some evidence to suggest that formal instruction may have the effect of hastening the acquisition of this sequence (Ellis 1989, Pienemann 1989).

c: Some language forms are clearly more learnable than others. For instance, Pica (1985) points out that the acquisition of features like plural 's' can be enhanced by formal instruction. It seems that certain language forms are more teachable because they bear a real and immediate relationship with real life referents.

All this suggests that even if it was possible to make all input in the mainstream classroom comprehensible, it is not enough to leave language acquisition to comprehensible input. While there may be some fixed sequence of some syntactical structures, the acquisition of such structures can be speeded up by formal instruction. In any case, we know that language learners, particularly at the early stages, rely upon formulaic and holistic phrases, and these can certainly be taught (Hyltenstam 1985; Nicholas 1985; Widdowson 1989).

The demands of the National Curriculum

The National Curriculum requires all pupils to follow the prescribed programmes of study in the mainstream classroom. English as a subject in the National Curriculum expects all pupils to have knowledge of standard English and sociolinguistic and pragmatic aspects of language use, and to be able to apply such knowledge in appropriate contexts relevant to age and grade (Cox 1989). Second language pupils are, in the main, not exempted from this requirement. All pupils, irrespective of their language backgrounds, are expected to follow the full range of subjects in the National Curriculum in the mainstream classroom. We are now obliged to provide an effective second language pedagogy in the mainstream context. We need to develop an approach that will provide genuine language learning opportunities in the mainstream subject classroom, so that learners are engaged in content and language learning at the same time. For all intents and purposes, the subject syllabus is the language learning syllabus.

Greater equal opportunities

We turn now to some of the pioneering work on integrating content and language learning.

Snow et al (1989) draw a distinction between content-obligatory language and content-compatible language, and they suggest that it may be useful to think in terms of content-compatible language when preparing materials for second language pupils in the mainstream. Put briefly, "content compatible language objectives can be taught within the context of a given content, but are not required for successful content mastery. Whereas content obligatory objectives derive directly from the linguistic needs for communicating the information in the content area, content compatible language objectives derive from the second/foreign language curriculum and ongoing assessment of learner needs and progress" (1989: 205-6).

This approach requires the mainstream subject teacher and the second language teacher to work closely together, developing materials which are informed by subject specific content and the second langauge needs of the learner. At this stage it is not very clear to us how to decide what content compatible language is. In a lot of cases, learners might have a range of needs, and we cannot respond to them all at the same time. We need, therefore, to work out a more precise and helpful way of deciding what is content compatible language. Nevertheless, we feel this is a useful conceptual distinction, which helps us to focus more sharply on second language pedagogy in the mainstream. (For a related discussion see O'Malley 1988).

Another way of approaching this issue is to look at subject topics as a series of tasks. Conceptually, tasks are at the same level of realization as units/topics within a paticular course of study, e.g. the design of a picture frame in a Creative Design and Technology class. The tasks are dictated by the subject content, but the tasks themselves form the basis of the real moment-by-moment and lesson-by-lesson language syllabus. The subject teacher and the second language teacher will need to concern themselves with both
a) what is achieved through teaching and learning using the existing competence of the learners in performing particular tasks; and
b) what is to be learned in terms of language forms and pragmatic use which will help develop and expand the language learner's repertoire up to the level required.
In sum, the language teacher in the mainstream classroom not only has to deal with continuously changing subject-based tasks, but also a language content which has to take account of the changing tasks and changing learner competence.

Mohan (1989) suggests that the integration of subject content and language learning may be achieved by using graphics to represent the underlying knowledge structure of the subject content material. The graphics which express the content ideas can then be used to support and guide learners' written or oral work. These diagrams and pictures may be produced by the teacher, or by the pupil, or by both jointly. Pedagogically, this seems a very elegant way of enabling second language learners and teachers in the mainstream subject classroom to focus more clearly on the content learning task and the language learning task.

We feel that both the task-based approach and the use of graphics are practicable ideas for the mainstream classroom. But before these ideas can be properly translated into practice, a set of contextualised working guidelines must be developed for both initial and in-service training. It would also be important to monitor and evaluate the outcome of any attempt to put these ideas into practice.

Finally, we would like to emphasise that we also need to take into account the pragmatic aspect of language use, if we are to develop a more effective second language pedagogy in the mainstream. An exclusive concern with the formal properties of English will not satisfy the demands of the National Curriculum. Any future discussion on the development of second language pedagogy will need to encompass the notion of communicative competence, and to build on the large amount of work that has already been done in this area, especially the work of Canale and Swain (see Davies 1989 for a recent review).

Conclusion
During the last ten years, second language pedagogy in the UK has been primarily concerned with moving children into the mainstream. We support the general movement towards mainstreaming, but we have argued that not enough attention has been given to pedagogical considerations in this mainstreaming process. It is simply not good enough to put second language learners in the mainstream classroom and expect them to acquire the target language. There is enough evidence from recent research to suggest that teaching DOES matter. The principal concern for all second language teachers must be to enable second language learners to become independent and successful langugae users in their own learning. We are calling for greater effort to develop a more effective model of second language practice in the English mainstream context. The most urgent question now seems to be how to integrate language and content within the National Curriculum.

REFERENCES

BOURNE, J. 1989. *Moving into the mainstream: LEA provision for bilingual learners.* Windsor: NFER-Nelson.

BULLOCK. 1985. *A Language for Life.* The Bullock Report. London: HMSO.

CALDERDALE. 1986. *Teaching English as a second language.* The Calderdale report. London: Commission for Racial Equality.

COX. 1989. *English for ages 5 to 16.* The Cox report. London: HMSO.

DAVIES, A. 1989. Communicative competence as language use. *Applied Linguistics* 10,2 157-170.

DULAY, H, M BURT and S KRASHEN. 1982. *Language Two.* Oxford: Oxford University Press.

ELLIS, R. 1989. Are classroom and naturalistic acquisition the same? *Studies in Second Language Acquisition* 11, 305-328

GASS, S. 1988. Integrating research areas: a framework for second language studies. *Applied Linguistics* 9,2 198-217

GREGG, K. 1984. Krashen's monitor and Occam's razor. *Applied Linguistics* 5,2 79-100.

HYLTENSTAM, K and M PIENEMANN. 1985. *Modelling and assessing second language acquisition.* Cleveland: Multilingual Matters.

KRASHEN, S. 1981. *Second language acquisition and second language learning.* Oxford: Pergamon.

KRASHEN, S. 1982. *Principles and practice in second langugae acquisition.* Oxford: Pergamon.

KRASHEN, S. 1985. *The input hypothesis: issues and implications.* Harlow: Longman.

KRASHEN, S. 1988. *Second language acquisition and second language learning.* London: Prentice-Hall.

LEUNG, C, and C FRANSON. 1990. Teaching English as a second language in the mainstream classroom: collaboration, not co-presence. *Journal of Further and Higher Education* 14,3

MOHAN, B. 1989. Knowledge structures and academic discourse. *Word* 40, 1

NICHOLAS, H. 1985. Learner variations and the teachability hypothesis. In: Hyltenstam and Pienemann (eds).

O'MALLEY, J. 1988. The cognitive academic language learning approach. *Journal of Multilingual and Multicultural Development* 9,1.

PICA, T. 1985. Linguistic simplicity and learnabilty: implications for language syllabus design. In: Hyltenstam and Pienemann (eds) 1985.

PIENEMANN, M 1985. Is language teachable? Psycholinguistic experiments and hypotheses. *Applied Linguistics* 10,1 52-79.

SHARWOOD-SMITH, M. 1986. Comprehension vs Acquisition: two ways of processing input. *Applied Linguistics* 7,3 239-256

SWAIN, M. 1988. Manipulating and complimenting content teaching to maximise second language learning. *TESL Canada Journal,* 6,1

SWANN. 1985. *Education for all*. The Swann report. London: HMSO.

WHITE, L. 1987. Against comprehensible input: the input hypothesis and the development of second language competence. *Applied Linguistics* 8,2 95-110.

WIDDOWSON, H. 1990. *Aspects of language teaching*. Oxford: Oxford University Press.